Thomas Hodgkin

Narrative of a Journey to Morocco

In 1863 and 1864, With Geological Annotations

Thomas Hodgkin

Narrative of a Journey to Morocco
In 1863 and 1864, With Geological Annotations

ISBN/EAN: 9783744799751

Printed in Europe, USA, Canada, Australia, Japan

Cover: Foto ©Andreas Hilbeck / pixelio.de

More available books at **www.hansebooks.com**

OF A

JOURNEY TO MOROCCO,

IN 1863 AND 1864,

BY THE LATE

THOMAS HODGKIN, M.D., F.R.G.S.,

WITH

GEOLOGICAL ANNOTATIONS.

London:
T. CAUTLEY NEWBY, PUBLISHER,
30, WELBECK STREET, CAVENDISH SQUARE.
1866.
[THE RIGHT OF TRANSLATION IS RESERVED.]

IN CONFORMITY

WITH THE EXPRESSED DESIRE

OF THE LATE

DR. THOMAS HODGKIN,

THIS VOLUME IS

DEDICATED (BY PERMISSION), TO

SIR MOSES MONTEFIORE, BART.,

BY HIS HUMBLE AND OBEDIENT SERVANT,

THE PUBLISHER.

List of Subscribers.

List of Subscribers.

	COPIES.
H.R.H. the Prince de Joinville, Lansdowne Villa, Richmond	1
The Honble. Lady Hotham	1
Sir Moses Montefiore, Bart.	20
Sir James Clarke, Bart., Bagshot	1
Sir Roderick Impey Murchison, Bart., K.C.B., President of the Royal Geographical Society	1
Adler, Rev. D., Chief Rabbi, 16, Finsbury Square	1
Alsop, Robert, Esq., 36, Park Road, Stoke Newington	1
Alexander, Mrs. Ann, Ipswich	5
Allen, Richard, Esq., Sackville Street, Dublin	1
Armytage, Captain, R.N.	1
Ashby, Thomas, Esq., Staines	1
Adams, William, Esq., 5, Henrietta Street, Cavendish Square	1

LIST OF SUBSCRIBERS.

	COPIES.
Albright, Arthur, Esq., 30, George Street, Egbaston, Birmingham	1
Alger, John, Esq., Sydney, New South Wales	1
Ashby, Mrs. Charles, Staines	1
Ashworth, Henry, Esq., Bolton	1
Bassett, Francis, Esq., Leighton Buzzard	1
Braithwaite, Isaac, Esq., Austin Friars	1
Braithwaite, J. B., Esq., 312, Camden Road	1
Backhouse, Mrs. Katharine, Darlington	1
Bergne, Mrs. De, 17, Palace Gardens	2
Bell, Thomas, Esq., F.R.S., The Wakes, Selbourne	1
Bassett, John Dollin, Esq., The Cedars, Leighton Buzzard	1
Bevan, Paul, Esq., Tottenham	1
Bryant, William, Esq., Surbiton, Surrey	1
Brewin, W., Esq., Cirencester	1
Barclay, Mrs. Eliza, Blackwell, near Darlington	1
Bowly, Mrs. Elizabeth, Cirencester	1
Bell, Miss Eliza, Borovere, Alton, Hants	2
Ball, William, Esq., Bruce Grove, Tottenham	1
Backhouse, James, Esq., Holgate House, York	1
Binns, Mrs. S. H., Hoddesdon	1
Burgess, Mrs. Susanna, Ridlington Park, Uppingham	1
Crawford, Lieutenant-General, 36, Prince's Gardens	1

LIST OF SUBSCRIBERS.

	COPIES.
Clulow and Son, Messrs., Derby	1
Cohen, Mrs., Asgill House, Richmond	1
Cadbury, James, Esq., Banbury, Oxon	1
Callan, Miss Isabella M., The Camels, Wimbledon Park	1
Coutts, Miss Burdett, Holly Lodge, Highgate Rise	1
Christy, Edmund, Esq., 35, Gracechurch Street	1
Christy, J. F., Esq., 35, Gracechurch Street	1
Christy, Alfred, Esq., 35, Gracechurch Street ...	1
Christy, Wakefield, Esq., 35, Gracechurch Street	1
Christy, Miss Ann, Woodbines, Kingston-on-Thames	3
Christy, A., Esq. ...	1
Cox, Mrs., Lawford Place, Manningtree	1
Charleton, Robert, Esq., Ashley Down, Bristol	1
Daniel, James I., Esq., Ramsgate ...	1
Dimsdale, Mrs. Elizabeth Gurney, St. Paul's Square, York	2
Davis, Alfred, Esq., Norfolk Hotel, Norfolk Square, Hyde Park ...	1
Driver, Mrs, 6, Sumner Place, Onslow Square	1
Darby, Mrs. Alfred, Stanley Hall, Bridgnorth	1
Driver, Mrs. Louisa, Highbury Park	1
Doncaster, Mr. Daniel, junr., Sheffield	1
Ecroyd, William, Esq., Lomeshay, Burnley	1

LIST OF SUBSCRIBERS.

	COPIES.
Feltham, Miss, Roseville, Winchmore Hill	1
Fry, Edward, Esq., 6, The Grove, Highgate	1
Fuller, D. P., Esq., Sion Hill, Ramsgate	1
Ferguson, Mr., Liverpool	1
Fowler, Mrs. L., Tottenham	1
Frith, Mr. Thomas, Toothill Rastrick	1
Goodbody, Jonathan, Esq., Clara, King's Co.	3
Guedalla, Henry, Esq., 9, Devonshire Terrace, Hyde Park	1
Gay, John, Esq., 10, Finsbury Place, South	1
Gregory, James, Esq., Evesham, Worcestershire	1
Gillett, Jonathan, Esq., The Elms, Banbury	1
Grubb, Mrs. Anna, 27, Gloucester Road, Regent's Park	1
Gompertz, Mrs, 1, Upper Kennington Lane, Vauxhall	1
Galloway, R. H., Esq., 27, Hyde Park Square	1
Godlee, Rickman, Esq., Lillies Upton, Essex	1
Gill, Henry, Esq., Oxford Lodge, Croydon, Surrey	1
Godlee, Burwood, Esq., Lewes	1
Hodgkin, John, Esq., The Shelleys, Lewes	4
Heymann, L., Esq., West Bridgford, Nottingham	1
Howard, Robert, Esq., Tottenham	2
Hodgkin, Thomas, Esq., Newcastle-on-Tyne	5
Hanbury, Cornelius, Esq., Wellington, Somerset	1

LIST OF SUBSCRIBERS.

	COPIES.
Hull, Mrs. A. M., Uxbridge	1
Howard, W. H., Esq., St. Thomas', Exeter	1
Horniman, John, Esq., Coombe Cliff, Croydon	1
Hawley, Mrs., 26, Highbury Grove	1
Harrison, Miss, 10, Chapel Place, Ramsgate, Kent	1
Horne, Miss M. A., Clapham Common	1
Hull, Samuel, Esq., Uxbridge	1
Hills, Mr. W. H., Bookseller, Sunderland	2
Hudson, Scott, and Son, Booksellers, Carlisle	1
Howard, Mrs. E., Bruce Grove, Tottenham	1
Hewitson, Miss H., Woodlands, Headingley	1
Houghton, G. P., Esq., Cork	1
Harding, R. Esq., Great Henny	1
Hadwen, H., Esq., Ashfield, Lancaster	1
Harper, A., Esq., 26, Highbury Place	1
Harvey, Mr. Thomas, Leeds	1
Kursheedt, Mrs., Sussex Gardens	1
Kempe, G. J., Esq., Beechwood, Rochdale	1
Kitchin, Dr., Enfield	1
Lucas, Joseph, Esq., Oakfield, Hitchen, Herts	1
Lister, Joseph J., Esq., Upton, Stratford, E.	2
Loewe, Dr. L., 46 and 48, Buckingham Place, Brighton	1

LIST OF SUBSCRIBERS.

COPIES.

Lucas, Mrs. Philip, Edinburgh (late of Temple House, Manchester)	1
Levy, Alexander, Esq., 28, Finsbury Square	1
Lister, W., Esq., 11, Somers Place, Hyde Park	1
Lamley, Mr. R., Tredington	1
Mocatta, F. D., Esq., 35, Gloucester Place, Portman Square	1
Montefiore, T. M., Esq., 4, Great Stanhope Street	1
Montefiore, A. J., Esq., Thanet House, Highbury New Park	1
Mussy, H. Guineau, Esq., M.D., 4, Cavendish Place	1
Morley, Samuel, Esq., Wood Street	1
Masterson, the Misses, Clarence Villa, East Cowes Park, Isle of Wight ...	2
Müller, Mrs, 7, Grosvenor Gate, Park Lane	1
Moses, H. L., Esq., Cornwall Terrace, Regent's Park	1
May, Edward Curtis, Esq., Bruce Grove, Tottenham	1
Morland, H. John, Esq., Heath Lodge, Croydon	1
Mudie, C. E., Esq.	50
Nunes, W. A., Esq., Colonial Office	1
Nichol, Mrs. Elizabeth P., Huntly Lodge, Merchiston, Edinburgh	2
Norton, Thomas, Esq., Peckham Rye Common	1
Newham, Samuel, Esq., The Park, Nottingham	1
Norton, Thomas, Esq., Peckham Rye	1

LIST OF SUBSCRIBERS.

	COPIES.
Parken, W. P., Esq., St. Albans	1
Peckover, Algernon, Esq., Wisbeach	2
Prier, Miss Mary, 21, York Place, Brighton	1
Pope, Mrs. Margaret, Staines	2
Pryor, John, Esq., 17, Bedford Square	1
Peile, George, Esq., Whitehaven ...	1
Pease, Henry, Esq., Stanhope Castle, Darlington	1
Pattison, Miss Helen C., 11, Montague Place, Russell Square ...	1
Pattison, Frederick, Esq., 11, Montague Place, Russell Square	2
Pim, Miss Priscilla, Wandsworth...	2
Pease, John B., Esq., North Lodge, Darlington	1
Richardson, James, Esq., Elswick Leather Works, Newcastle	1
Richardson, Mrs. Edward, South Ashfield, Newcastle-upon-Tyne	1
Rickman, Mrs. Hannah, Birkenhead	1
Roslin, Samuel, Esq., Reading	1
Rowntree, William, Esq., Scarborough	1
Richards, Mrs., 10, Victoria Road, South Kensington	1
Rowntree, Joshua, Esq., Scarborough	1
Rowntree, John, Esq., Scarborough	1
Ransome, R. C., Esq., Orwell Lodge, Ipswich ...	1
Ransome, —, Esq. (Ransome and Sims) Ipswich	1

LIST OF SUBSCRIBERS.

                                                                       COPIES.

Richards, Oliver, Esq., 5, Clarendon Road, Victoria Road, South Kensington 1

Rees and Gripper, Messrs., Booksellers, Ipswich   1

Rickman, Miss Sarah H., Lewes 1

Smith, Mrs. G. M., 10, Highbury Place   1

Sturge, Miss, 27, Duncan Terrace, Islington ... 1

Smith, Richard, Esq., 7, Highbury Crescent ... 1

Sebag, Joseph, Esq., 38, York Place 1

Scriven, S. S., Esq., F.R.C.S., Southdown, Weymouth, Dorset 1

Sampson, Samuel, Esq., 23, Tavistock Street, Gordon Square 1

Stephenson, Miss Mary, 41, Great Russell Street   1

Sharples, Joseph, Esq., Hitchin 1

Shewell, Mrs. Elizabeth, relict of John Talwin Shewell, Rushmere, near Ipswich 1

Shewell, Joseph, Esq., Colchester 1

Schwerin, Mrs. Caroline, 7, Grosvenor Gate, Park Lane ... 1

Strachan, J. S., Esq., Lodgemore Mills, Stroud ... 1

Samuel, S. M., Esq., 29, Park Crescent, N.W. ... 1

Shephard, Mark Holman, Esq., Mount Road, Blossom Street, York 1

Smith, E. Pye, Esq., Hackney, N.E.   1

Southall, Rittson, Esq., King's Acre, Hereford ... 1

Session, Mr. W., Bookseller, York ... 1

LIST OF SUBSCRIBERS.

Thompson, Miss, Colebrook Terrace, Islington	1
Thompson, Miss Emily, Colebrook Terrace, Islington	1
Thompson, Miss Mary, Colebrook Terrace, Islington	1
Thompson, Edward, Esq., Rydal House, Highbury New Park	1
Taylor, the Misses, Aden Terrace, Stoke Newington	2
Tweedy, Mrs., Truro, Cornwall	1
Tuckett, Philip Debell, Esq., Frenchay, near Bristol	1
Theakstone, S. W., Esq., Scarborough	1
Tuke, H., Esq., M.D., 37, Albemarle Street	1
Tatham, W., Esq., M.D., Melton Mowbray	1
Travers, Miss M. T., Wyvol's Cottage, Swallowfield, Reading	1
Travers, Miss, Hillingdon Cottage, near Uxbridge	1
Whitehead, Thomas, Esq., Eastcheap, E.C.	1
Williams, Caleb, Esq., M.D., York	1
Warner, Charles B., Esq., Crescent, Jewin Street	1
Wilson, William, Esq., Sherwood Hall, Mansfield, Nottinghamshire	1
Wilson, John E., Esq., Augustus Road, Birmingham	1
White, W. Foster, Esq., Bartholomew's Hospital	1
West, L. Heymann, Esq., Bridgford, Notts,	1
Ward, John I., Esq., Stock Exchange	1
Wallis, Charles, Esq., Basingstoke	1
Wright, Mr. James, Bookseller, Sudbury	1
Yates, James, M.A., F.R.S., Lauderdale House, Highgate	1

PREFACE.

PREFACE.

Some few days before the late Dr. Thomas Hodgkin left England on his last sad journey to Jerusalem, he called [...] cript of this [...] gements for [...] ies respecting [...] ng the work, [...] thers that he [...] namely, that [...] u Sir Moses

ERRATA.

In page 47, line 8, for "ramiform" read "reniform."

In page 48, 5 lines from the bottom, for "calcedony" read "chalcedony."

In page 97, 6 lines from the bottom, for "T. M. Reade" read "T. F. Reade."

In page 140, line 15, for "were" read "was."

The irreparable loss which Mrs. Hodgkin sustained was communicated to her by H. Guedalla, Esq., nephew of Sir Moses Montefiore, who had received a telegram from Jerusalem, giving the fact of Dr. Hodgkin's death on the 4th of April at Jaffa.

* It should be mentioned that the Manuscript, when shown to the publisher, was in a very crude condition, a fact named by the author at the time, who also stated that it was his intention, before placing the work in the hands of the printer, to carefully revise the whole. Unhappily he did not live to accomplish his intentions, which melancholy circumstance will account for any inaccuracies which it is feared may be found in the volume.

PREFACE.

SOME few days before the late Dr. Thomas Hodgkin left England on his last sad journey to Jerusalem, he called upon his friend the publisher with the manuscript of this volume, for the purpose of making arrangements for its publication, as well as to state his wishes respecting the sketches which he had made for illustrating the work, and to talk over other minor details.*

There was, however, one desire above all others that he particularly requested might be accomplished, namely, that the publisher should obtain permission from Sir Moses Montefiore to dedicate the volume to him.

The irreparable loss which Mrs. Hodgkin sustained was communicated to her by H. Guedalla, Esq., nephew of Sir Moses Montefiore, who had received a telegram from Jerusalem, giving the fact of Dr. Hodgkin's death on the 4th of April at Jaffa.

* It should be mentioned that the Manuscript, when shown to the publisher, was in a very crude condition, a fact named by the author at the time, who also stated that it was his intention, before placing the work in the hands of the printer, to carefully revise the whole. Unhappily he did not live to accomplish his intentions, which melancholy circumstance will account for any inaccuracies which it is feared may be found in the volume.

The first written communication of the melancholy tidings was to John Hodgkin, Esq., of Lewes, in a letter from Capt. Moore, a military officer, who formed one of Sir Moses Montefiore's travelling party. It was dated,

"Jerusalem, 10th April, 1866.

" . . . As you are probably aware, Dr. Hodgkin complained of feeling ill the morning we left Alexandria, and the voyage to Jaffa seems to have done him no good. At Jaffa, he continued ailing, and, as he did not seem to improve, Sir Moses sent for Dr. Chaplin, of Jerusalem, and, that gentleman having assured Sir Moses that the symptoms were not dangerous, he (Sir Moses) being most anxious to reach Jerusalem for the approaching Passover, left his friend with the greatest reluctance. . . . . After making him as comfortable as possible in the house of the officiating Consul, Mr. Kayat, a most excellent and amiable young man, we started for Jerusalem, with the Doctor's full consent.

"On the third day after our arrival, an alarming telegram was received from the Italian doctor in attendance. Sir Moses at once sent for me to express his great concern at not being able to go down to Jaffa himself, and be near his sick friend; at the same time intimating a wish that

I should go down to Jaffa, which I at once did, accompanied by Dr. Chaplin; and after riding all night, reached Jaffa about nine, a.m., and found the poor doctor, as reported, in a dangerous state. Inflammation had set in, and his malady had assumed the form of acute dysentery.

"The poor doctor seemed glad to see us, and, although I did all in my power to reassure and encourage him, he would not admit he was not in a dying state. The doctors, although fully aware of the gravity of his case, did not give up all hope.

"During this time, his sufferings were often most acute. I feel sure that you will rejoice to hear that he bore them with the utmost fortitude and resignation, praying that the will of the Lord might be done, and saying, 'He has given and He has taken away,' and 'Blessed be His name.'

"I myself cannot find words to express my profound admiration at the calm attitude of this most excellent man and Christian in the hour of trial and suffering . . . . His last thoughts were of his Maker and the eternity opening before him. He prayed to be allowed a few hours' respite from pain before the final struggle, a request which I have every reason to believe was granted. He passed away calmly.

"Dr. Hodgkin expired at a quarter past five in the evening of the 4th of April, and was buried in the English cemetery, near the city walls, outside the new gate, and nearly opposite the British Consul's house. The funeral was attended by the few Protestants residing at Jaffa, the officiating Consul, and the people attached to his office, with the two doctors and myself, and two European attendants left with him by Sir Moses.

"It was a lovely morning, but most sad and mournful was the group which stood around the grave of your dear brother and their lamented friend. A strong wooden railing has been put around the grave, to mark the spot for the present, till a suitable monument can be sent from Europe.

"With every good wish,

"Pray believe me,

"Dear Sir,

"Yours very truly,

(Signed) "HENRY MOORE."

A few days after the receipt of Capt. Moore's letter, Mrs. Hodgkin had one from Mr. H. A. Kayat, dated,

"Jaffa, April 14th, 1866.

"MADAM,

"It is with feelings of deep grief that I have to execute the painful duty of acquainting you that it has pleased the Almighty to call unto Himself your dear husband, my good friend, the late Dr. Hodgkin.

"When I wrote to you by last mail, there was little hope left, and now we must resign ourselves to his will. 'Blessed be the name of the Lord;' these were the last words that I heard from the mouth of the departed. His thoughts were fully directed and fixed upon eternity; his faith was firm. For about a week before his death he was very weak, and in a sinking state; he then seemed to think he was past recovery. He was fully resigned; indeed, it was impossible to have evinced more Christian patience than he did, never repining, never murmuring, though enduring the greatest pain.

"The two medical men that were in attendance, Drs. Chaplin and Loggi, did all they possibly could, and there was no lack of anything for his comfort in my house. But alas! the malady was so virulent, that it prostrated and carried him off. For about half-an-hour before his end he was free from pain; then he departed calmly and in peace, on Wednesday, the 4th of April, at five p.m.

"'He surely sleepeth in Jesus.' 'Blessed are the dead that die in the Lord.'

"May the Lord give you peace and comfort.

"Believe me,

"Dear Madam,

"Most truly yours,

(Signed) "H. A. KAYAT."

The most treasured document which Mrs. Hodgkin received, was a letter dictated by her husband, only three days before his death, in which occur the following words:

"My dear love to all my friends. I lament the little service which I have done, and I entreat all to love and serve their Lord and Master.

"The last two days at Alexandria knocked me up; the weather was oppressive. I have been in almost ceaseless agony, and the sufferings consequent upon my disorder have worn me down.

"Dear Sir Moses was obliged to leave me, to go to Jerusalem; but he has been boundless in his kindness, and spared nothing for my relief."

Dr. Chaplin, of Jerusalem, by desire of Sir Moses Montefiore, twice visited Dr. Hodgkin professionally at Jaffa, and remained with him till his death. On the 17th of April he wrote a letter to Mrs. Hodgkin, from which the following are extracts:—

"He was quite conscious almost to the last. He prayed much and spoke often to me of the state of his mind. He said: 'Difference in religious persuasion need not separate us. We are brethren in Christ, and Christ is not divided.'

"It seemed a comfort to be able to speak fully upon these topics. I asked him if he would like the English Clergyman from Jerusalem to visit him. He said: 'No; it is not in numbers. If my Omnipotent Lord is with me, that is all the comfort I need.'"

As soon as the first shock occasioned by the death of Dr. Hodgkin had somewhat subsided, an anxious desire was expressed by several of his intimate friends and admirers, that his "Narrative of a Journey to Morocco" should be published, and that it should form a handsome volume, embellished with a portrait of the author and with some of the sketches he made when on his journey, thus making a "Memorial Volume," in which the names of the friends and admirers of the author might be inserted as a tribute of love and respect to his memory.

It would be out of place in a volume like this to attempt anything in the shape of a Biography, or to record the innumerable benefits to society resulting from the unwearied zeal and the enlarged mind and heart of Dr. Thomas Hodgkin, for they are engraven on the hearts of all who knew him.

It will, however, be universally acceptable to give the following "Obituary Notices," which appeared in the public journals, showing as they do, that not only was he esteemed for his domestic virtues by a numerous body of relatives and friends, but that he was equally valued as a public benefactor.

The "Morning Star," in a rapid Biographical Sketch adds :—

" The death of any man who has devoted himself with unwearied zeal to works of practical beneficence, who has employed all his powers of heart and intellect in the service of mankind, and especially of one who, in addition to his more public work, exhibited personal virtues which made him an example and a blessing to his fellow man—the death of such a man is nothing short of a public calamity. The late Dr. Hodgkin was an Englishman of this type. His only ambition was to do good ; thoroughly unselfish and single-minded, he preferred to live for others instead of for himself; and thousands dwelling in many lands will deplore his untimely death, although they only knew him by his labours on their behalf.

"He undertook two journeys to the Holy Land with Sir Moses Montefiore, with the view of assisting in various schemes of benevolence, more especially designed for the benefit of the Jewish people. He also repeatedly accompanied that generous and philanthropic Israelite in other journeys, including an arduous one to Morocco in 1864, for the purpose of an interview with the Emperor, which was crowned with remarkable success, in procuring the rescue of several Jewish prisoners, and establishing liberty of conscience, both for Jews, and indirectly for Gentiles also, in that Mohammedan empire. It was on the second of the above-mentioned journeys to the Holy Land that his decease took place. No sketch of his character would be complete which omitted to notice his widely-diffused and genial, though simple hospitality. His house was the rendezvous for representatives from almost every nation under heaven, and though this was occasionally taken advantage of by men who were unworthy to share his friendship, we have reason to know that in many other instances it was the means both of bringing unappreciated merit into notice, and of promoting a kindly feeling towards England in the hearts of foreigners."

From the "British Medical Journal" of April 28th, 1866, the following extract will show the high esteem in which Dr. Hodgkin was held by the profession of which he was so distinguished a member:—

"There can be but few, if any, men in the medical profession who have been more universally esteemed than Dr. Hodgkin, or who have more thoroughly deserved respect. In times past a hard-working and able pathologist and physician; always, and especially in late years, a sincere and judicious promoter of the good of his fellow-men; an accomplished scholar, and a consistent Quaker and Christian, Dr. Hodgkin has passed away, while engaged in one of those philanthropic enterprises, which were most congenial to him.

"In the world of science, Dr. Hodgkin will be remembered as one of the pioneers of pathology in Great Britain, and as an accomplished and observant physician. Among men of all nations and all callings, wherever his name becomes known, it will be received and treasured in remembrance as the name of 'One who loved his fellow-man.' "

By the Israelitish people the death of Dr. Hodgkin has been considered a public calamity. The "Jewish Chronicle" of September 28th, 1866, contains a heartfelt and beautiful tribute to his memory, in the subjoined letter, from the pen of Israel's veteran champion, Sir Moses Montefiore, in his report to the Board of Deputies:—

"It has pleased the Almighty to take him (Dr. Hodgkin) from us, and that he should not again behold his loving consort and beloved relatives. He breathed his last in a land endeared to him by hallowed reminiscences. To one so guileless, so pious, so amiable in private life, so respected in his public career, and so desirous to assist, with all his heart, in the amelioration of the condition of the human race, death could not have had any terror. His soul has ascended to appear before the throne of glory, there to receive that heavenly recompense which is awarded to the good and righteous of all nations.

"I trust I may be pardoned for this heartfelt but inadequate tribute to the memory of my late friend. His long and intimate association with me and my late dearly-beloved wife, his companionship in our travels, and the vivid recollection of his many virtues, make me anxious to blend his name and the record of his virtues, with the narrative of these events."

With his accustomed kind feeling and liberality, Sir Moses Montefiore has sent an obelisk to be erected on the spot where the mortal remains of his attached friend rest, as a special memento of the reciprocal attachment that had existed uninterruptedly between them for a period of forty years.

The obelisk is of highly-polished Aberdeen granite.

THE EDITOR.

NARRATIVE OF A JOURNEY TO MOROCCO.

PRELIMINARY.

On the 31st of 10th month, seventh day, 1863, a packet of letters was received by Sir Moses Montefiore at his country residence, Eastcliff Lodge, Ramsgate; and as it happened to be his Sabbath, they were all opened for him. Thus, as we may believe, providentially, one of them, which would, in all probability, have been forwarded unopened to his nephew, Joseph M. Montefiore, instead of being delayed, obtained the immediate attention of Sir Moses. Its purport was of pressing importance. It came from some of the leading members of the Israelitish community of Gibraltar, who were thrown into painful sympathy with their brethren at Tangier, whom recent occurrences had placed in alarm and danger.

A Spaniard in Saffi, in the employ of his own government, or in the service of its Vice-Consul, had died so suddenly that suspicions of foul play, probably poisoning, were excited in the mind of the Spanish representative, who, in his official character, insisted upon the Moorish authorities investigating the case, and inflicting punishment on the guilty. No steps were taken to ascertain whether there were any facts to establish the cause of death, or show that it had any connexion whatever with crime; but, according to custom in Morocco, suspicious parties were sought and examined by very severe scourging, as well as by some other methods of torture. Israelites being the most unprotected of the population, a Jewish lad, about fourteen years of age, who resided in the family of the deceased, was the first person so examined. After long persisting in the assertion of his innocence, he yielded to the pressure of protracted agony, and declared that poison had been used. The influence of torture being still continued, ten or eleven other persons, whose names were suggested to the lad, were denounced by him as participators in the crime. Most of these were arrested, but one of them only was subjected to examination by torture. Though this measure was pushed to a fearful extremity, no crimination of himself or others could be wrung from him. The lad also, when released from torture, uniformly asserted his innocence.

However, as the lad had confessed and the man had been denounced, both were condemned to death, doubtless to prove the readiness of the Morocco Government to comply with the demands of its recent conqueror. The lad was accordingly executed at Saffi, the execution producing as its natural consequence great dismay amongst the Jewish population; but the man was conveyed in a Spanish vessel to Tangier. Nothing is known of the reasons which led to the adoption of this course, but it seems to be very probable that it was taken in order that the knowledge of the circumstance might be spread more rapidly and extensively through the Moorish dominions, from the principal emporium of the state and the chief residence of the foreigners representing their respective countries. This public execution, almost under their eyes, could not fail to impress these gentlemen with a striking idea of the magnitude of Spanish influence in the court of the Sultan. The alarm felt by the Israelites at Tangier was extreme, and, as has already been said, was forthwith communicated to Gibraltar.

Nine or ten individuals lay at Saffi, menaced with a fate like that of their two brethren. Sir Moses Montefiore's prompt and active benevolence was aroused to a high pitch, and early on the morning of the first day, 11th month, he was on his way to London, and by noon was hunting up the Secretary and Under Secretaries of the Foreign Department. Earl Russell was out of town; but though it was Sunday, Sir Moses succeeded in gaining an interview with the Under Secretary. Telegraphic communications were resorted to, and in a wonderfully short time the wires of the Continental telegraph were at work, conveying the instructions of the Foreign Office in London to Sir John Drummond Hay, the British Ambassador at Tangier, to use all the influence of his position to obtain at least a temporary suspension of further executions. Such was the cordial alacrity with which the British Government gave its important and timely assistance, that this despatch anticipated the telegram previously sent by Sir Moses by some hours.

An important pause in the proceedings being thus obtained, Sir Moses Montefiore, in conjunction with the Board of Deputies, maintained an active correspondence with their co-religionists in Gibraltar and Tangier, and deeply interesting circumstantial statements were received and translated. At this stage of the affair Sir Moses intimated to some of his associates on the Board of Deputies his willingness, if it should be thought desirable, again to make the sacrifice of his time and his home comforts to advocate, in person, the cause of his suffering brethren, and to proceed to Madrid, Tangier, and Saffi. The offer was hailed with approbation, and gratefully accepted.

It was finally concluded that Sir Moses Montefiore should have as his companion Sampson Samuel, the solicitor and secretary to the Board of Deputies, who was thoroughly conversant with the affairs of the Israelite body, and in particular cognisant of all that had transpired in relation to the occurrences which led to the mission. He was, therefore, well qualified to fill the post of secretary on this occasion. Hyam Guedalla, the husband of Sir Moses' niece, and as such, his personal friend, whose father was a native of the country, and as a merchant most extensively known in Morocco, with pleasure accepted his uncle's proposal to join him. I had also the privilege of forming one of the party, and as an old and attached fellow-traveller and friend, took a pleasing interest in endeavouring to maintain the health and strength of the venerable leader of the expedition, hoping that my exertions during a long journey, unavoidably attended with fatigue, difficulty, and not altogether without risk, would afford some satisfaction to Sir Moses' anxious relatives; besides which my own feelings were warmly engaged in the undertaking. Shalon Ferrache, who for several years had acted as courier to Sir Moses Montefiore when travelling in Palestine, Syria, Egypt, and on the Continent of Europe, was peculiarly qualified for the same post on this occasion, being himself a native of Morocco, in which country, as well as in Spain, he had been accustomed to travel, and being familiar with the languages of both countries. The personal convenience and comfort of Sir Moses was also well provided for by his taking with him Charles Oliffe, an old and faithful attendant, well known in the employ of the Alliance Assurance Office, and also Albertine Muller, a highly respectable native of Hanover, very familiar with all that can be required, either in sickness or in health, from a female attendant in travel.

TO MADRID.

OUR party assembled at the Lord Warden Hotel, Dover, on the evening of the 16th day 11th month, and early the following morning embarked in a steamer for Calais; a large assemblage of friends accompanying us to the pier, not only to take leave, but to express their hearty good wishes, the same having been previously marked in a more solemn manner in several synagogues in London and elsewhere. We arrived in Paris the same evening, where, from oft repeated visits, Sir Moses Montefiore found a home in Meurice's Hotel.

It was scarcely daylight the following morning when we were all in movement for the Station du Midi, and although Poictiers or Angoulême had been looked to as the possible resting-place for the night, the journey was continued to Bordeaux. After such an effort a period of rest was absolutely necessary. At Bordeaux Sir Moses had the pleasure of meeting David da Costa, an old friend of most of the party. He had formerly been superintendent of the large works at Marseilles belonging to the Imperial Continental Gas Company; but on its operations in that city being forcibly suspended, through the intrigues of M. Mirés and his party, David da Costa was transferred to the important works of the same company in Bordeaux. As one of the founders of this company, and its president, Sir Moses has taken a warm interest in its operations, and, when time and strength have permitted, he has, when visiting any of its establishments, carefully examined their proceedings technically and financially. Some attention of this kind engaged him even on this transient opportunity. He was likewise diligent in visiting and paying his respects to his brethren and co-religionists, individually and collectively. On the morning of the twentieth we proceeded by train to Bayonne; this journey, though short, presented considerable interest from the peculiar character of the district traversed, being that of the celebrated Landes; a wide-spread sandy plain, to the eye of almost boundless extent, and in most parts apparently nearly as level as water. Till comparatively of late years this tract had, from time immemorial, been almost exclusively devoted to pasturage, and the inhabitants, to enable them to inspect their flocks and herds, and perhaps also to facilitate their crossing ditches and marshes, were in the habitual practice of going about on high stilts. The herdsmen, often remaining for hours in this position, would fill up their leisure time in knitting stockings. In the present altered circumstances of the country, stilts seem to be laid aside. We looked out for them almost in vain. One old man, past work, was seen standing on them and knitting, but he appeared like a relic preserved for show. A few boys might also be seen amusing themselves with their miniature stilts. The reclamation of this tract, both in tilling and planting, has been very rapidly and profitably advancing, and from all that I could observe, in twice quickly crossing it in a railway carriage, I have no doubt that it offers much more for interesting examination than might at first be expected from the nature of the country. Pines appear to flourish admirably, and to grow with great rapidity. In many places the cutting of timber is going on so largely that the air is perfectly scented with it. It is not the wood alone that pays the planter, for at the proper season of the year turpentine is collected in great abundance in numerous small vessels placed to receive it below the notches made in the tree for its escape.

This turpentine, highly esteemed, both for the essential oil and the resin, has greatly increased in value and demand since the commencement of the war in America. From the greater attention given to its collection, it is said to be far superior to the American turpentine.

Cork is also produced in this district, and here, as in other situations in which cork trees are profitably grown, I noticed that the bark of other trees also is unusually thickened. As far as I have been able to discover, the soil in cork districts is sandy, and frequently derived from the *débris* of porphyry.

At a considerable distance before arriving at Bayonne, the surface of the country becomes much more undulating, and Dax is seen at a short distance to the left. There is a station for its convenience, but no opportunity occurred for visiting this ancient town. It is considered to be a remarkably well-preserved specimen of the early period at which it flourished, and as such its antique walls, once devoted to destruction, are still preserved, for which it is understood that thanks are due to the present Emperor. In commemoration of this fact, a medal has been struck by the distinguished English Archæologist, Roche Smith, who for its execution engaged his able and ingenious countryman, W. J. Taylor, of London.

We arrived in very good time at Bayonne, but Sir Moses, who in this hasty journey maintained the incognito, had given no intimation of his coming. His arrival, however, could not remain a secret. Whilst taking advantage of the daylight to look about the town, I was accosted by an Israelitish gentleman, who, I know not why, discerning I was of Sir Moses' party, politely plied me with questions to ascertain the fact, which I as studiously, but courteously, endeavoured not to divulge. The secret, however, was not long kept, for in the course of the same afternoon I met the same gentleman (M. Leon) at our hotel, and then commenced an acquaintance with him and several members of his family. Their unremitting, zealous, and liberal attentions and valuable assistance merit our warmest and most grateful acknowledgments. Not only did the thoughtful care of M. Leon provide us with excellent animal food, of which the majority of our party could partake, and which, travelling in Spain, they might have sought in vain, but he would willingly have devoted himself to have accompanied us throughout the mission.

At Bayonne, Sir Moses rested on the 21st of the 11th month for the Sabbath, and I profited by the opportunity to visit the noted little town of Biarritz. Besides the Imperial residence and some other public buildings, several lodging-houses have been recently erected, which give the town almost the appearance of an English watering-place. English notices are seen in the shops, and the door-plate of an English physician emboldened me to ring the bell and make the acquaintance of the occupant, whom I found a very agreeable and intelligent gentleman.

On the 22nd of the eleventh month, partly by rail, and partly by diligence, we pursued our journey to San Sebastian, to which place we were accompanied by M. Leon and several of his relatives. The road is in some places sufficiently near the shore to be in sight of the sea; in others, passing through and over a pass of the Pyrenees, afforded us beautiful and magnificent views. The curious and interesting old town of St. Jean de Luz is on this route, many of the houses of which are no less remarkable for their architecture than for the historical facts with which they are connected. Near this place is a small island, on which was celebrated the marriage of Louis XIV. with the Infanta of Spain. At St. Jean de Luz, there are also considerable remains of an ancient bridge, of Roman work.

The small basin and harbour, communicating with the sea by a narrow but deep cleft from the hills, is peculiarly striking and picturesque. It does not seem capable of admitting vessels of large size.

At Irun, a frontier town on the Spanish side, we met with a long detention, caused by the general inspection of the passengers' luggage. The railway at this part was not then completed, and there were several vehicles besides our own pressing forwards to the nearest railway station.

During this detention I walked to a short distance, and obtained a view of the noted little town of Fuenterrabia, beautifully situated at the southern side of the bay.

But little daylight remained when we arrived at the San Sebastian station, built on the large plain to the north of the town. This open space serves as a promenade, on which a considerable concourse of persons, in their Sunday dresses, were enjoying the evening of their holiday. As we walked into the fortified town, several spots, rendered interesting by the awful and sanguinary siege from which the place severely suffered towards the close of the Peninsular war, were pointed out to us by our companions.

It was soon too dark for us to obtain much of a view of the town, but as I was desirous to find the residence and make the acquaintance of Antonio Brunel, who had resided for some time in England, I sallied forth. In this walk I noticed a number of young persons collected about a musician, some of whom were dancing, and I was told that the dance was peculiar to the Basques, of whom the inhabitants of this portion of Spain and of the adjoining part of France mainly consist. Of the dance I could form no opinion. I regretted having so transient a view of this interesting people. The town itself is much improved since the siege, and contains several streets of good houses.

We were ready to depart very early in the morning, and before daylight were at the railway station, accompanied not only by our kind friends from Bayonne, but also by Antonio Brunel, of San Sebastian, who came to our hotel to see me.

It is needless to describe the journey from San Sebastian to Burgos. As it was night before we arrived there, and as we left it again some time before sunrise, we could scarcely be said to have seen the city, though we had a glimpse of its cathedral and of the fortifications on the hill before our train left the station. It is a good day's journey from Burgos to Madrid, where Sir Moses arrived on the evening of the 24th of the 11th month (November). Having been accidentally left behind by the premature departure of the train from Avila, whilst I was endeavouring to obtain a view of the town at a little distance from the station, I was unavoidably detained for several hours, there being no train till past midnight. There is much to interest in this curious old town, but being without guide, interpreter, or handbook, I did not obtain all the gratification which I might have done from this untoward circumstance. The town is situated in the midst of a granitic district. The walls, churches, and houses are constructed of granite, and the streets are in many places paved with very large blocks of the same material; but notwithstanding the durability of the granite, the paving is in bad order. The cathedral, which is close to the city wall, is, even for a Spanish church, remarkably dark and gloomy within, and the access to the interior is so intricate that, having entered, I had considerable difficulty in making my escape from its gloomy solitude. There are several other churches, both within and without the walls, and one of the latter in particular, which does not appear to be in use at present, struck me as presenting some notable architectural peculiarities. The granite walls of Avila are not very lofty, and have many projections or bastions, which stand out considerably, forming oblong rather than semi-circular towers. The huge bare and more or less rounded granite rocks, scattered in every direction and in vast profusion, give a peculiar character to the appearance of the surrounding country. The sandy soil, produced by the disintegration of the granite, is, of course, but little fertile, and where trees are to be seen they are, except in the immediate vicinity of Avila, almost exclusively of a species of pine, or dwarf evergreen oak.

The refreshment room of the Avila station was kept by a Frenchman and his family, and the genuine civility and kindness which they cordially exhibited to an English traveller, accidentally left amongst them, deserves to be gratefully remembered. As the train did not reach Madrid till about nine o'clock, it was bright and clear daylight when it passed the Escurial, and I had a fine, though somewhat distant, view of that extensive and remarkable pile of buildings, an advantage which my friends had lost by having passed it late in the evening.

Sir Moses Montefiore took up his residence at the Hotel de los Principes, Puerta del Sol, the most desirable situation in Madrid, where he remained from the 24th of the 11th month (November) till the 1st of the 12th month (December), and the whole of this time he was sedulously and anxiously engaged in endeavouring, by conciliation, to promote the object of his mission. This large, fine, and constantly-increasing capital forms a striking contrast with almost everything else we saw in Spain. Its elevated position gives a deep blue sky, which during the time of our visit was often nearly cloudless, and, notwithstanding the period of the year, the rays of the sun were really powerful, though the winds were cold and searching.

Sir Moses Montefiore received from Sir J. F. Crampton, the British Ambassador to the Court of Spain, all the kind and cordial attention which his own well-known character and the warm introduction of the Government which he represented, could not fail to inspire. Their interviews were frequent, both at the British Embassy and at the hotel. Visits were paid to and received from the Marquis of Miraflores, the Prime Minister, the Duc of Tetuan, General Prim, and other persons of distinction, to whom he was not only introduced by the British Ambassador, but also by his private friend and relative, Mr. Weisweiller, who had long resided in Madrid, and whose high position as an important financier, and the Consul of more than one foreign country, as well as his amiable disposition and great liberality, rendered him highly influential, even with the Court itself.

Although these introductions were the means of procuring for Sir Moses the most friendly feeling on the part of the Queen's Ministers, and distinct assurances that the recent proceedings in Tangier had not been dictated by any unkindness or prejudice on their part, as well as letters for the Spanish Minister at Tangier, written expressly for the purpose of facilitating his object, he was unwilling to quit Madrid until he had had a personal interview with the Queen herself. Circumstances unavoidably occasioned delay in this taking place, but Her Majesty having appointed the 28th for the audience, which was subsequently deferred till the 30th (November), Sir Moses was introduced by Sir J. F. Crampton to the Queen and her consort at a private audience, which lasted a considerable time, and must have been agreeable and satisfactory.

MADRID.

I met with very little in Madrid to interest me, as it is not a city which possesses many of those objects which suit my taste. I repeatedly saw that good man Luis Uzos y Rio, with whom I was much pleased, but we did not have long interviews.

A curious plan is adopted here of not permitting the museums to be opened unless the day be fine, and a cloudy sky with small rain prevented my gaining admission. I went out for the purpose of visiting the Veterinary College, but finding its locality had just been changed, I did not attempt to go to the new one. The finest portion of the picture gallery was also shut, so that I was not fortunate in obtaining the inspection of the little which is worthy of attention.

Being near the building where the bull-fights take place, I looked into it. It very much resembles an old Roman amphitheatre, from which it is doubtless derived; but it is greatly inferior, for though the few lower rows of seats are of stone and have the same kind of access as the ancient models, the major part is only of wood, and instead of the fine vaulted corridors there are only miserable passages. Even these are too good for the object, and I trust that this disgrace to the national taste is going out of vogue. Neither the Queen nor her consort encourages these amusements, and fewer women go than formerly. Two of our party went to an exhibition of the kind yesterday afternoon, which, being out of the season, was designed to be a mild affair, the bulls' horns being sheathed, or otherwise rendered less likely to hurt. It was, however, a repulsive and disgusting sight, and one or two animals were killed.

I went to the hospital, and though it was closed, the hour being late, I was permitted, through the politeness of the medical attendant, to see some of the wards. This morning I went to the observatory, but did not go in. From the height upon which it stands there is nothing particularly striking to be seen on a dull day, except a pretty extensive view of the city and the outline of the mountainous horizon, near which we catch a view of the distinct truncated conical height wrongly regarded as the centre of Spain.

SANTA CRUZ DE MUDELA.

THE twelfth month (December) commenced at Santa Cruz de Mudela with beautiful weather, for although it rained a little it was in general quite fine, and the thermometer stood at nearly seventy. The day had often been cloudy, but the sky, where clear, had a fine blue, the effect of our standing very high. We were, in fact, on a high and remarkably level plain, which seems to have been formerly a lake, the sandy alluvium, where occasionally cut into, being to appearance perfectly horizontal. At first the hills which bounded our view formed table land, with occasional breaks, the truncated conical sandhills rising somewhat like those about Shandon, but nearer the place where we halted they are more pointed. We started about half-past six o'clock, and stopped a little before four in the afternoon, having arrived at the place where the railroad ceases and diligence travelling is still continued. We might have gone on almost immediately, but this would have necessitated travelling through the night, which would have been very unsuitable for Sir Moses, added to which a kind friend of his at Madrid had taken the pains to send beforehand ample instructions for our reception, and also to provide beds, &c., &c.

On arriving, I took advantage of the daylight to inspect the little town about a mile from the station, and which I suppose is a fair specimen of an unchanged, ordinary Spanish town. It is not walled, the streets nearly straight, tolerably wide, and where they cross each other it is nearly at right angles. Very few, if any, of the houses have more than one story above the ground floor, and in most instances, the rooms above the ground floor must be little better than lofts. Few houses have proper glazed windows. Instead, the small opening has externally an iron grating, and in some instances, and when not quite open, the closure is by a shutter, in which a small pane of glass is inserted. The streets have very much the appearance of those in some of the worst Irish towns. The walls are of various materials, stone, brick, and mud; walls of the last description are not unfrequent for gardens and orchards. A clean and neat appearance is given by the whitewash, which is very general, and seemed to have been freely and recently used; and the stone, tile, or pebble floor, which I could see from the doors, which were mostly open, appeared well swept; and I remarked that this was also the case with the narrow pitched footways; but the horseways were in many places deep in mud and ruts. The females, in many of the houses, were seated at the wide open doors, engaged at needle work, or knitting. They were generally tolerably dressed; but the labouring men were very roughly clothed, and instead of shoes and stockings, had whitish, coarse linen, bound rudely about their feet and legs. A little before entering the town, I noticed an ass working in a circle, to turn a wheel, charged with buckets, which, as they revolved, emptied themselves into a trough, in precisely the eastern style. Having to rise very early, the whole party retired sooner than usual, and we were, with our effects, settled in the diligence, and in motion, about five o'clock, on the morning of the 2nd. We speedily crossed the mountains which border the plain, on which we had travelled the preceding day; but soon after descending, we were again ascending, and were crossing the Sierra Morena, at the summit of which pass the aneroid barometer stood at 27 inches. This chain bounds Andalusia on this side, and we immediately observed a change in the productions of the country, and in the active occupation of its inhabitants. The fields are better cultivated. The olives most extensively so; and though vast numbers appear to be excessively old, there are many young olive yards. The trees are planted in rows, and extend to the tops of the smaller hills. We passed, at least, one lead mine. About four in the afternoon, we arrived at Andujar. Sir Moses Montefiore had received a letter at Madrid, introducing him to M. Fragneau, chief engineer of the railway operations, and every arrangement was made for his and our good reception; but H. Guedalla and I thought it best to go on with the diligence to Cordova, where we arrived about midnight. Sir Moses Montefiore left Andujar the following day, and joined us late at night.

CORDOVA.

CORDOVA is a city of large size, on the Guadalquiver. It boasts a doubtful origin to a *very* early period; but its authentic age is sufficient to make it venerable. It certainly existed under the Roman Empire; but acquired its greatest celebrity under its Mahometan masters. It still retains much of a Moorish character, even in things not necessarily Mahometan. By far the most remarkable object is the cathedral, which is well worth seeing, even after St. Peter, St. Paul, St. Sophia at Constantinople, or any of the Mosques there or in Egypt. I cannot state its actual dimensions; but whilst the proportions of St. Peter's are such as to make the beholder, on his first visit, somewhat lose the appreciation of its vast size, those of this building are calculated to produce just the opposite effect. Except in a tolerably large and nearly central space devoted to the high altar, the height is by no means proportionately very great; and eight hundred and sixty columns of marble and granite, forming avenues, and supporting Moorish arches, produce an effect something like that of a pine forest. The original colour of the interior has generally been defaced by whitewash. The doors, and probably windows also, which suited it as a Mosque, have been closed to form chapels round the sides of the building within. Semicircular, gothic, and other arches and architectural features, have been introduced, besides the greater changes in the internal arrangement, to which I have adverted, in the formation of the part devoted to the high altar and its accompaniments, which I will not attempt to describe, except by saying they are very rich, though not in keeping with the original work. There are two or three parts of the Moorish edifice still remaining remarkably intact, which are extremely rich, and probably give a better idea of Saracenic art at its highest period, than anything which I have seen in Constantinople or in Egypt. I refer especially to a portion said to be that in which the Caliphs worshipped; and to another portion now railed off, and forming a kind of chapel, in which the remains of a Spanish General are interred. The inscriptions, almost *Kufic*, the rest mosaic, and the intricate, deep carving, resembling filigree, are, I apprehend, unequalled, unless it be at the Alhambra.

Near one of the arches of the vaulted roof of the less elevated part of the Cathedral, is suspended an elephant's tusk, of rather small size. It is said to have been discovered on making excavations in the ground, in the interior of the building. I know nothing of the depth at which it was found, and I understand that different conjectures have been formed respecting it. I imagine that it may have been attributed to Carthaginians bringing elephants here, as they did into Italy, or to Saracens; but examining it, as well as I could, from a distance, I fancy that it may have been that of a wild elephant, to whom Spain was its native country, perhaps at a time when there were also native British elephants. Its cracks and dead whiteness favour this idea. I saw the Roman, and the remains of the Moorish bridges; the Caliph's palace, now a prison; the market, formerly a place for bullfights, a part of which still exhibits the boxes for the spectators; the remains of the Moorish walls, chiefly composed of earth, with a little stone and brick casing, and having several towers; a church, in which are the tombs of Ferdinand, a Castilian king, and his son, Alphonzo; and also that of a celebrated writer, Morales. I noticed, projecting into the river, what appeared to be a mass of stonework, looking very like the foot of an old bridge, but when I came closer it appeared like a number of square foundations, the object of which I could not understand and the guide could not explain. However, he asked an elderly gentleman, who was near, who told us they were the remains of pits formerly used in the preparation of leather. Shortly after, and still by the waterside, I saw a skin of black shoe leather hanging up, and on examining it I thought of a kind of leather which I heard spoken of when I was a boy, and called Cordevan by the shoemakers, and which name was said to be derived from Cuir de Van. This, however, was evidently of sheep's skin, and I suspect that Cordevan was a corruption of Cordovan. The general use of whitewash, which I noticed at Santa Cruz de Mudela, prevails at Cordova, as well as in other places through which we passed. Several of the local peculiarities are seen better here and in a more marked manner than in many or perhaps any other place. Thus, the houses have generally a comparatively small apartment without furniture, upon which the street door opens, whilst another door, usually of open iron work, or sometimes a curtain, such as may have formerly been adapted to a tent, separates it from the rest of the house, so that it forms a spacious and commodious internal porch. To most of the houses, which are sufficiently large, there is an inner court with columns round it, as in cloisters. Within the court are flowers, and round it are apartments which open into it. The representations of the Alhambra and of Pompeii at the Sydenham Palace give a tolerable idea of them. The shops are very different from those of England, France, &c. Perhaps most of them expose little or nothing at the window; but the counter fronts the customer at his entrance, and the shelves with goods are behind. Not unfrequently attractive goods are placed at the doors.

CADIZ.

Sir Moses did not find himself equal to start by the early train for Seville, we therefore had part of another day at Cordova. This gave me an opportunity of crossing the bridge, and walking about on the other side, which I had not previously done. I also examined the broad shore of the Guadalquiver, where, as I suspected might be the case, I found the large supply of water-worn boulders with which the streets, courts, and even floors of houses are paved. They are of various sizes and colours, and consist of green stone, porphyry, and quartz; the alluvial soil of the district is also full of them.

The pigs in this country are remarkably fine, and I could not help standing for some time to admire a herd of them basking on the sandy and pebbly shore, doubtless rendered warm by the bright sun. They were fat enough for prize animals, but not so disgustingly unwieldy and flabby as those exhibited at the English shows. They looked clean, not being confined to styes, and having their troughs near them they were not tempted to ramble. They thus had the full benefit of fresh air, so conducive and necessary to health. This example affords one of a few hints which may be taken in England, even from Spain.

Having been obliged to defer our journey to Seville to the second and last train, our arrival on the 6th was very late. Sir Moses delivered the letter of introduction to Don Antonio Merry the next day, and received from him one to his son, Don Francisco Merry y Colon, the Spanish Minister at Tangier. We left Seville on the 8th, by railway, and arrived at Cadiz late the same night. Sir Moses was much fatigued, and had greatly increased a very troublesome cold. He was confined to his bed on the following day.

On our way to Cadiz we passed through the sherry district, but as it was dark I can say very little about it, except that soon after leaving Seville, we passed a wood of rather lofty pines, without leaves or branches, except near the summit, which formed roundish heads, somewhat like mops. I think they must be allied to those called umbrella pines. The region is, with some exceptions, a complete level. We passed the port of St. Mary, where much wine is shipped, and we had for a fellow traveller a young Englishman who resides there, and is in the wine trade.

TANGIER.

SIR MOSES heard, it would seem providentially, that the French steam frigate "Gorgone" was about to sail on the evening of the 10th for Tangier direct, and as there were no means of an immediate transit to Gibraltar, he at once forwarded a request to the Commander, Capt. Cellier de Starnor, to allow our party to take passage in his ship. This was most promptly and politely acceded to. Capt. Starnor, an amiable man, seemed pleased to show his hospitality, and we received every attention and accommodation. We left Cadiz on the night of the 10th day, at 10 p.m., and arrived off Tangier at five a.m. the next morning. Sir Moses's arrival had been anticipated and well prepared for, a large concourse of people being ready to receive him. There is no pier at Tangier, and the water being shallow off the coast, passengers have to be carried, and there was a multitude in the water—some wading nearly up to their waists—waiting to bear us to the shore. We did not land until about eight o'clock.

Our kind captain and his officers had ingeniously contrived, on the spur of the occasion, by the help of a mattrass and cordage, a kind of portable couch or car, on which, for want of a suitable landing-place, Sir Moses might be borne over a considerable extent of shallow water between the boat and the shore. His porters and a great many of the labouring class of Israelites were wading, and his superior size thus conspicuously moving over the water, surrounded by a shabby, amphibious group, appeared to me like a travestied representation of Neptune among the Tritons. The rest of the party were carried on shore by some of these waders, who were provided with chairs for the purpose, and it was fortunate that none of the travellers were upset and well ducked, in the vigorous struggles that were made to obtain a passenger.

Rather a steep and not well-paved road leads into the town, over which Sir Moses had to pass to reach the best hotel in the place, which is kept by a Scotch hostess.

The whole party were closely thronged by a vast number of Israelite population from the town, of all classes and both sexes. This afforded us the first opportunity of hearing the peculiar sound uttered by the Jewish females in Morocco when they wish to give expression to their joyful greetings with distinguished honour. We had been fully apprised of the hospitable design of our Tangier friends; but Sir Moses Montefiore was not dissuaded from his original intention of taking up his residence at an hotel until, on arriving there, the earnest solicitations of M. Moses Pariente, seconded by those of his fellow citizens, prevailed upon him to go to the far more commodious accommodation afforded in this gentleman's house, which had been vacated and expressly fitted up for the occasion. It was an excellent specimen of Tangirene dwellings, being, like most of them, situate in a narrow street or lane, the principal entrance leading into a quadrangular court, round which the apartments are arranged, forming two stories, and in part a third, the doors of the upper apartments opening upon a gallery with a railing to it, as in many of the old English inns. The staircase is continued to the roof, which being flat and surrounded by a high parapet is much resorted to, especially by the females, who thus have the benefit of the air without exposure in the streets. The roof and the walls being white-washed, have a very bright and neat appearance. This house, like many others in the town, has upon the roof a portion erected above the rest, from which a more extensive view may be commanded. We were soon settled and refreshed in these comfortable quarters, and in a very short time introduced to the heads of the Israelite community.

Whilst Sir Moses, his nephew, and secretary were thus engaged, I took advantage of a beautifully fine day to look about the town, having for my guide the brother of our courier, whom I had previously seen in England. Tangier lies in a valley, between two hills, the houses being thickly placed on their sides, so as to leave a more extensive vacant space between them, which serves both for a market-place and a principal ascending street, leading to the back of the town. In this street, besides many small shops, are some of the best houses, occupied by the officials of different European powers and other Christian inhabitants. In the market-place and shops a great variety of articles attract the attention of a stranger, either as new in themselves, or with some novelty in the mode of exposure. Capons, turkeys, and other poultry are cooped in cylindrical cages, made of reeds, or placed on the ground, tied together by the legs. The varieties of grain, beans, and other seeds are also numerous. Considerable quantities of bread, in flat loaves resembling Bath cakes, but of much larger dimensions, appear to be brought, ready baked, from the country by swarthy peasants of both sexes, who perseveringly offer them for sale. Then we have dates and other dried fruits, and the kernels of walnuts and other nuts, removed from their shells. The soap of the country is also a conspicuous article. It is soft and of a dark colour, and if seen in England, in a druggist's laboratory, would undoubtedly be taken for tar ointment. The candles also attract attention, being remarkably conical, from eight or nine inches to a foot in length, perhaps nearly two inches in diameter at the base, and tapering very regularly almost to a point at the top. This form, which is nearly as exact as if made in a mould, is, I understand, produced by the mode of dipping whilst they are attached to a vertical rotating wheel. I did not, however, witness the manufacture.

Quitting the main street, and turning to the right or west, we ascended, by a winding and steep path, to the Fort, or Governor's residence, with several official buildings about it. One, I understood, was used as a prison; others appeared to be mosques, and some were, doubtless, the residence of the soldiers, their horses being tethered by their fore feet in the walled yards, without any shelter or litter. This fort occupies nearly or quite the entire summit of the western hill; and the damage done to its walls by the guns of the Royal Fleet of France still remains unrepaired, and very conspicuous. At the fort forming part of the city wall, in this direction, there is a good Moorish gateway, through which, on quitting the town, we came upon gardens, fields, and a more or less wooded country. On the summit of the hill, facing the sea, and commanding a beautiful view of the coasts of Africa and Spain, are private gardens, or rather hanging gardens, with enclosed apartments or summer houses; they appear to belong to the wealthy inhabitants, who resort to them for their pleasure. We happened to meet one of our hospitable Jewish friends who opened the door of one of them, and I thus had the opportunity of inspecting a good specimen of these pleasant retreats.

Descending the hill on the outer side of the town, we came upon the large, open, elevated space, which is situated at the upper extremity of the central street before mentioned; here the larger quantities of grain and more bulky articles are exposed, and here also are collected the numerous camels which bring to Tangier the productions of the interior, Fez, Mequinez, and perhaps even of Timbuctoo. The sight, however, was by no means calculated to confirm ideas produced by the somewhat poetical descriptions which are given of the ship of the desert. I had seen camels before in Egypt and Palestine, which had, in a degree, obliterated such an impression; but I was not prepared to behold such wretched animals as I found in Tangier; they had probably but recently arrived from a long journey, and many of them were not only miserably thin, but sadly wrung and sore from the pressure and friction of ill-adjusted burdens; some were decidedly pugnacious, and others by no means tractable. These animals, when arrived at their journey's end, are, like the horses, mules, and asses, put up in large walled enclosures, without litter or shelter.

Outside the walls near this part of the town, are pens or enclosures for beasts of various descriptions collected for sale, amongst which I noticed very lean cattle, poor horses, and a few pigs—apparently of the black Spanish breed—but widely differing from them in condition, being remarkably thin. Near to the gate by which the town is entered, on this side, is the place where horses appear to be brought for the purpose of being shod; and without attempting to describe the process, I may just observe I was forcibly and painfully struck with the liberal use of a kind of adze, with which the foot is chopped, rather than cut or pared, to prepare it for the application of the shoe. Various races and costumes are, of course, to be met with in Tangier; and in this first walk a poor, thin, ill-clad negro pilgrim from Timbuctoo was pointed out to me.

The peasants from the immediate neighbourhood wear the white woollen burnous, with which the women, for the most part, nearly conceal their faces. Many of the native residents, as well as Europeans, adopt the European costume, whilst several others, even of the wealthier class of Israelites, wear a kind of tunic, generally blue, and bearing some resemblance to a dressing gown. In Tangier, at least, they seem, for the most part, to be exempt from any restriction in this respect, although the case of several Israelites would indicate that before our arrival this freedom was rather tolerated than recognized round Tangier.

This first and hasty survey afforded me much material for reflection, and I shortly after committed my ideas to writing, and although my subsequent increased acquaintance with the Sultan's dominions furnished me with numerous additional facts, the opinions which were then suggested are rather confirmed than altered.

Sir Moses Montefiore received deputations from the Israelites of Tetuan, Alcazar, Arzila, Laraish, and Mequinez, which afforded him much gratification; also addresses from his co-religionists of Mogador, Azamor, and Fez. On the twelfth he attended Divine service in the new synagogue, erected by M. Joseph Eshriquy, who dedicated the sacred edifice for the benefit of the poor, in commemoration of the Mission.

Sir Moses waited on Sir J. H. D. Hay, K.C.B., the British representative, on the next day, meeting Consul-General Ranger, and received a kind reception; and afterwards, accompanied by Sampson Samuel, he delivered the letter of introduction to Don Francisco Merry y Colon, and other letters he had received at Madrid. His reception by the Spanish Minister was most courteous, resulting in the immediate release of two Israelites confined at Tangier, Jacob Benharrosh and Shalom Elcaim, who, within an hour of the interview, called at our residence.

A letter to the Moorish Government was also promised respecting the two prisoners at Saffi. This was received the next day before noon, and a visit was paid to Sid Mohammed Bargash, the Minister for Foreign Affairs, upon the introduction of Sir John H. D. Hay.

Upon our return to our quarters, we found a large deputation of Moors, about fifty in number, with their chiefs, who had come from a distant part of the country, to urge Sir Moses to intercede for the release of one of their tribe, who had been imprisoned for two years and a half, on suspicion of having murdered two Israelites, but had not been brought to trial. As his guilt had not been proved, and as he had for so long a period endured the horrors of a Moorish prison, it was not surprising that Sir Moses was quite ready to make a humane effort on his behalf—one as politic as it was congenial to his kind disposition, since, if successful, it could scarcely fail to have the effect of producing a favourable feeling on the part of this man's tribe towards their Israelite countrymen. His intercession was promptly undertaken, and equally promptly successful; in a few hours the prisoner's chains were removed, and he was brought by the members of his tribe to return thanks to his deliverer. He was a middle-aged man, above rather than below the average size, of a fair complexion, and by no means of a repulsive countenance. He was in good condition, and in a state of health, which did not indicate suffering from confinement, being well washed, and clothed in a clean woollen burnous; he had a really respectable appearance. His innocence of the crime imputed to him was strongly insisted upon by himself and his friends.

Sir Moses Montefiore did not lose the opportunity to urge these grateful Moors to shew kindness and afford protection to his co-religionists; and they readily gave their solemn promise that all Jews travelling by day should be perfectly safe.

During our sojourn at Tangier, Sir Moses Montefiore's attention was called to the state of the schools, supported by the Israelite community, for the education of their youth. We frequently had the company of Solomon Israel, a very intelligent young man, who had been educated at Gibraltar, where he had been instructed in the management of schools. On him devolved the chief care of giving instruction in the English language, which, in many respects, is more important to the interests of this portion of the empire of Morocco, and to the Jewish population in particular, than any other foreign language, not excepting the Spanish, which, however, is far more generally understood.

Notwithstanding the evidence of careful attention paid to the education of Jewish youth, it seemed not improbable that the Moorish custom of neglecting the education of females might, in some degree, affect the Israelite girls of the poorer class, and Sir Moses' solicitude on their account inspired him with the benevolent idea of founding a school for them. To promote the establishment of such an institution, he gave a donation of three hundred pounds, in memory of his late wife, Lady Montefiore, on the express condition that the regulation should be strictly under the control and superintendence of a ladies' committee, fully at liberty to seek the counsel and assistance of gentlemen when necessary. Before his departure, he had the satisfaction of knowing that several Jewish ladies had consented to act upon these conditions.

Most, if not all, of the Israelite families in Tangier had been visited once or oftener by our whole party, which gave us the opportunity of enjoying their hospitality, and of seeing good specimens of Moorish dwellings, many of which were well supplied with European furniture and ornamental works. So much kindness made Sir Moses feel that he could do no less than endeavour to entertain an evening party in return. Two or three rooms of good size were really crowded with a lively company of both sexes and various ages. The Jewish females enjoy a privilege which may well excite the envy of their Mohammedan neighbours, since they appear to be under no painful restraint in these social entertainments. Such at least was our experience in Tangier, but other visitors to the north of Morocco have given a somewhat different account. The Jewesses are far more personable than the other women of the country, whom we had the opportunity of seeing, and many of them are really beautiful. It is not an uncommon practice amongst them to apply powdered antimony to their eyelashes and edges of the eyelids. This produces a curious effect, which, though admired by some, is not, in my opinion, in the least degree ornamental. Their nails and the extremities of their fingers are not unfrequently stained as in Egypt and Palestine, but instead of the brownish tint of the henna, a dark, or nearly black, colour seems to be in vogue.

I am a poor observer and worse describer of female attire, nevertheless the rich dresses worn at our evening party struck me as well deserving notice, and I give a few words respecting them, though necessarily defective in technicality. In the first place I may observe that I am not aware that the genuine effect of the folds of drapery was in a single instance vitiated by the interference of the European fashion of thin iron hoops, known by the inappropriate name of crinoline. The rich materials, if I am not mistaken, chiefly composed of silk, appeared however to have a certain degree of stiffness of their own, which was manifestly increased by the large amount of gold lace, which was very conspicuous in contrast with the ground, generally of a green colour, upon or into which it was embroidered. I cannot pretend to describe the pattern so produced, but a very common effect was that of portions of large concentric circles, the centres of which appeared to be at the bottom of the front of the robe. I am unable to describe the various head-dresses, and can only say that in brilliant gaiety they were quite in accordance with the other parts of the dress. Knowing that several precious stones are amongst the native productions of Morocco it was more in my way to notice the jewels worn by our guests, and it appeared to me that emeralds were the stones most abundantly worn, and I thought many of these gems appeared to be antiques.

To vary our entertainment a short lecture was given for the purpose of exhibiting a few experiments, chiefly chemical, necessarily limited by the scantiness of the materials we had with us, but with the help of a little chloride of potass, phosphorus, nitrate of silver, muriate of cobalt, nitrate of strontian, &c., the attempt was not altogether unsuccessful. I was less fortunate in my endeavour to make a few electrical experiments by the help of a machine constructed for the occasion out of a wine bottle, as shown to me fifty years ago, when a school boy, by Lord Overstone. This failure taught me one fact, which may be worth recording. My Tangier apparatus, though hastily put together, was in some respects more complete than my rough puerile work, which had been completely successful; but though the cylinder revolved truly and the rubber pressed evenly, though the amalgam was good and the silk clean, and the well insulated prime conductor by no means to be complained of, not a spark could be obtained, and the Leyden vial, well coated within and without, of course remained useless. Every attention to secure the most favourable circumstances produced no improvement, and after much waste of time the attempt was abandoned. The only reasonable explanation which I could conjecture for this defeat was that the bottle employed had not been merely blown but had received its form from a mould, which had produced a slight but almost imperceptible roughness. In the introductory remarks which preceded this little exhibition I took the liberty to introduce a few suggestions, which, whilst they

showed the interest I felt for those amongst whom I had been so kindly received, might, I thought, prove an assistance and encouragement to some of their young people. A Spanish translation had been made to facilitate its comprehension by the majority of those present. During our subsequent stay at Gibraltar my partial friend, Sir Moses Montefiore, paid me the compliment of having it printed in both languages, in order that it might have some circulation amongst his co-religionists in Morocco.

On the morning of the 22nd day, 12th month, we arose early, and a large number of the Israelite community assembled at our quarters, when a religious service of great length occupied a considerable time, and it was ten o'clock before we were under weigh. There had been much wind and rain during the night and early morning, but the weather cleared, and it was really fine when we departed. As in landing, we had to be carried by men wading into the water to reach the boats which took us to the steamer. The captain of this vessel had met Sir Moses twenty years before, and they soon recognised each other. He was a remarkable man, having very narrowly escaped death by shipwreck, when all on board except himself and a boy were lost. I understood they were some days at sea, and kept from sinking by the help of a plank, the man supporting the boy upon his back. For this act of persevering humanity he received a medal from the Humane Society, and other testimonials of public approbation. The distance from Tangier to Gibraltar is said to be about thirty miles, but it did not appear to me to be so much, the interesting coasts of Africa and Spain probably beguiling the time, and the clearness of the atmosphere diminishing the apparent distance. Turning Europa point, and steering up the beautiful bay, leaving Tarifa and Algeciras at our left, we saw many ships at the extremity of the bay. The place of landing is not far from the celebrated battery called the Devil's Tongue. There was quite a crowd, chiefly consisting of Israelites, assembled on the pier to receive us, and the guard on duty turned out and presented arms. The heads of the synagogues were there with carriages to convey us. Sir Moses said, "Let us go to the synagogue and return thanks." We drove to the principal, which was very soon completely filled; thence we proceeded to the good quarters which had been provided for us beyond the gates of the town in the quarter called the south, and just above the convict prison, and commanding, from its front windows, a capital view both of the bay and town. A troop of running men and boys accompanied us, and several carriages full of the chief members of the Jewish community followed. We assembled in the drawing-room, where an address was presented and read to Sir Moses, who, in reply, made one of his happiest speeches. Our kind and hospitable friends had been long expecting us, and the preparations which they had made for our accommodation were excellent. As a mark of honour and respect, a military band came in the evening and played before the house for a considerable time.

In good time next morning Sir Moses went to the Government House, which, from its original destination, is still called "the Convent," to pay his respects to Sir William Codrington, the present Governor, with whom, as well as with his father and brother, he had been previously acquainted. His whole party accompanied him on this occasion.

Sir William Codrington is decidedly popular, and deservedly so; particularly with the Jewish population, in whose hands is a large portion of the trade of the place, many of whom are understood to be wealthy. There is almost daily communication between Gibraltar and Tangier;

and the Israelite families in both places are, in many instances, united by family ties. During the late war between Morocco and Spain the Jews of Morocco were in great alarm, if not in actual danger, and fled to Gibraltar, where, for want of sufficient accommodation, many had to be encamped without the town. For this they had not only Government permission but assistance, and rations were distributed to them. The Governor showed them much kindness, and personally inspected their wants and saw to their relief. On the occasion of Sir Moses Montefiore's visit he invited some of the Israelite residents to meet him at dinner, which, as it was probably the first instance of the kind, must have been really gratifying to all parties.

Sir Moses Montefiore was zealous and indefatigable in attendance on the synagogues and giving audiences to deputations and individuals; he likewise visited several of the British residents, official and private, and I must particularly mention the chief artillery officer—under whose auspices we paid a visit to the galleries cut in the rock, which are amongst the principal wonders of the place—Captain, now Admiral Ommaney, whose elevated residence towards the southern extremity is perhaps the most beautiful in Gibraltar, and can scarcely be surpassed—and Admiral Codrington, the brother of the Governor, whose residence, not quite so elevated, commands a fine view. The side of the rock towards the bay, along which the town and fortifications are extended, is much less precipitous than that which rises from the Mediterranean, and it is, to a considerable extent, covered with trees, shrubs, and a variety of plants; at the period of our visit it was really verdant with numerous and large patches of brilliant colours.

GIBRALTAR.

During my first visit to Gibraltar my kind friend, C. Elliot, introduced me to Captain Broome, the superintendent of the prison at Windmill Hill, who had for a considerable time devoted careful attention to the exploration of an extensive and irregular cavern, formed by a fissure crossing the rock towards its south-western extremity. This cavern had been accidentally discovered whilst making the excavations that were necessary for the extension of a tank for the service of the enlarged prison. I was shown numerous portions of skeletons of various animals, intermixed with which were some human remains, manifestly of great antiquity. The collections of these objects were rapidly increasing under the assiduous care of Captain Broome, his colleagues, and the workmen engaged in the building department. A case of them had already been sent to the College of Surgeons in England, and others, which I had the pleasure of inspecting, were about to be forwarded thither. The impressions which I then received were hastily committed to paper in a letter to a friend. Conducted by the same able guide I subsequently saw most of the other caves in the limestone rock at Gibraltar, amongst which I must especially name that of St. Michael, rendered notorious by its having at one time concealed a numerous band of Spaniards, who had bound themselves under a solemn engagement to take Gibraltar, from the English, and restore it to their Sovereign. This cave is of very considerable dimensions, and descends, somewhat circuitously, to a great depth, expanding at intervals into spacious and lofty chambers, in which are numerous stalactites and stalacmites. Some of them are of very large dimensions, having a slight resemblance, though inferior, to those of the celebrated cave at Adelsberg. At the bottom there is a large accumulation of water, said to be connected with the sea, which intercepts the progress of the visitor, and I believe the full extent of the cave has not been yet ascertained. This, like the smaller caves, obviously owes its origin to the violent rupture of the rock and to the displacement of the detached portions. It is evident that rain-water penetrating the cavern from above often brings with it alluvium and vegetable mould, by which the stalactites are much disfigured, as well as considerable accumulations formed on the floor of the cave. As water, thus bringing with it various materials, is entering the cavern at various depths, it is obvious that whatever objects may be so introduced the time of their deposit cannot be inferred from the depth in which they are found, since some at the greatest depth may have been but recently imported, and even a covering of stalactite is not necessarily a proof of great antiquity.

I must not omit to state that through the kindness of my friend Elliot I had the advantage of seeing this really fine cave well lighted up. Without enumerating all the caves which had been discovered in the limestone rock of Gibraltar, I must revert to that which has been recently opened at Windmill Hill, which has received well merited attention, through the indefatigable labour of Captain Broome, under the auspices of the present Governor, Sir William Codrington. I learnt with pleasure that, since my previous visit, additional chambers had been discovered, and that the construction of the proposed tank had been interrupted and its original plan altered in order that this interesting exploration might not be seriously interfered with. The interest of the men employed in the work had been well sustained, and the objects brought to light had been carefully set apart, with accurate designation of the position from which they had been taken, on a plan resembling that employed by my friend Wm. Pengelley in the exploration of the cave at Brixham. It is needless that I should attempt to give any description of the numerous and varied animal remains, and of the specimens of early human art, which at the period of my visit had been discovered, since the whole collection up to a later period has been made the subject of the most careful investigation by my friend W. Busk, with the late lamented Dr. Faulkner, and the result obtained by these distinguished paleontologists will be duly recorded and published. I must, however, express my grateful acknowledgments to Captain Broome for the kindness and patience with which he enabled me to see and examine the work which he had already executed.

The warm interest which I could not fail to take in the investigations going forward on the Windmill Hill led to my having the pleasure and advantage of making the acquaintance of Sir James Cochrane and his family. Sir James has long been the Chief Justice of Gibraltar, and his residence in the southern quarter, at a lower level than the Windmill Prison, is situated over a cleft in the rock, which has produced a series of caverns, or clefts, of considerable extent, which, though they must have been known at a remote period, have, it seems, been lost sight of until recently re-discovered by workmen employed by Sir James Cochrane, who, on the discovery being made, pursued the exploration, and obtained fragments of human remains, which, however, do not appear to be equally ancient with those found at the Windmill Hill.

Day after day was passed, not without some

anxiety for the arrival of the frigate from Malta, yet, certainly, not without pleasure in the enjoyment of fine weather and much agreeable society. On the last day of the year, we were cheerfully seated at the dinner-table, in the evening, when a messenger came with a telegram. We, of course, joyfully expected an announcement of our coming conveyance; but our feelings were quickly changed, for, on opening the despatch, a few words expressed the sad intelligence that Sir Moses Montefiore's sister, Goldsmid, had expired at Nice. A short but severe attack of bronchitis had occurred, and Sir Moses was consequently wholly unprepared for so sudden and severe a blow as the death of a sister, to whom he was affectionately attached, and whose amiable character made her deservedly beloved by her relatives and friends. Her company as a fellow-traveller had added much to her brother's enjoyment, not many months before. Under any other circumstances than those in which he was then placed, Sir Moses would doubtless have lost no time in retracing his steps; but being on a mission of duty, he felt no hesitation as to the continuance of his journey. Our party, however, was to be separated, for it was quickly decided that Hyam Guedalla, the son-in-law of the deceased lady, should start, without delay, for Madrid, where it was presumed he might meet with intelligence to determine whether he should proceed to Nice or Paris. Sir Moses could not consent to his taking the journey alone, and insisted on surrendering Charles Oliffe, who had become a very useful travelling attendant, to accompany him on his homeward route. They started early the following morning, on board the steamer which plies between Gibraltar and Algeciras. From this place, another Spanish packet conveyed them to Cadiz, which proved a tedious and uncomfortable passage; but this was as nothing to the fearfully cold and trying journey which they experienced in going thence to Madrid. Their ink, and even their brandy and water, became frozen; and we might well congratulate ourselves that Sir Moses had come to the decision to remain quiet, instead of exposing himself to a risk, which, in the delightful climate of Gibraltar, we by no means anticipated. The arrival of H.M.S. Magicienne, from Malta, of which we were informed shortly after, gave us abundant occupation, and revived our spirits.

This frigate had been ordered by telegram, from England, to proceed from Malta, and to be placed at Sir Moses' disposal. The new Bishop of Malta, who had not as yet visited this part of his diocese, since his ordination, was on board. Though a good steamer, the Magicienne had made an unexpectedly long passage, having experienced a strong contrary wind. She was under the command of Captain Armytage, R.N., who had not long succeeded Captain the Prince of Leiuengen, R.N., the Queen's cousin.

A few days were required to collect and put on board the numerous articles necessary for our overland journey. Tents bedsteads, and bedding, besides lanterns and other utensils, were most carefully selected and prepared, of the description, best calculated to promote our comfort and convenience. Besides these, Sir Moses also purchased an ample supply of towels, napkins, cooking apparatus, &c., &c., as well as provisions of various kinds. This delay gave us an opportunity of becoming acquainted with the captain and some of his officers, who were about to be our fellow-travellers, and efficient co-operators.

As it was intended we should leave the port early on the morning of the 6th day, 1st month, we went on board over night, Sir Moses being lodged in the captain's cabin, adjoining the saloon, whilst Sampson Samuel and myself had our hammocks slung between two guns, next to the door of the captain's saloon, at which an orderly was placed on duty during the night.

Our kind companions spared no pains to render our voyage pleasant; and the captain's well furnished table was all that could be desired to counteract the aversion to food, inseparable from an Atlantic voyage, to those who are liable to sickness at sea.

To C. J. Forbes, the senior medical officer, and to — Durrant, the first lieutenant, who were our companions to Morocco, as well as by sea, we were more particularly indebted; but I must not omit to mention Dr. Lees, the second medical officer, an able draftsman, and other gentlemen, officers of different grades, who were remarkably kind, and impressed us with the belief that the service on board the Magicienne must afford a favourable specimen of the British navy. Beyond Cape Spartel the African coast, as seen from the sea, presents very little that is interesting, even when viewed from no great distance; but our course was frequently nearly or quite out of sight of land; even then, the nautical operations of the master and sailors, the practice of the midshipmen with their sextants, the guns, and other furniture of the ship, afforded abundant source of interest and amusement.

Besides Sir Moses Montefiore and his party, very few other persons were permitted as passengers on board the Magicienne; and only one of these had the advantage, besides ourselves, of the captain's table; this gentleman was Archibald Fairly, a civil engineer, who had been engaged in foreign service in India and elsewhere, and who was, like ourselves, proceeding to Morocco.

In the afternoon of the 9th day of first month (January), we arrived off Saffi, our progress having been delayed by contrary winds. Here, as at almost every port on the

West African coast, the landing is difficult, and the surf at the time was so high as to preclude the idea of our going on shore. The Magicienne saluted the fort with several guns, and the compliment was promptly returned. Recourse was had to signal flags, and by their assistance a sort of conversation was maintained with the town. To Sir Moses Montefiore's great satisfaction, he was informed that the prisoners at Saffi had been liberated; and the arrival of the Sultan's escort, destined to accompany us to Morocco, was also announced. The next morning the weather was fine and the sea much calmer. A few persons, chiefly Israelites, came on board from the town, and our courier, Ferrache, went on shore in one of the boats. In the prospect of our doing the same, a considerable part of our baggage was brought on deck; but the weather becoming again boisterous, we were obliged to put out to sea, though we did not altogether abandon the idea of landing.

From the sea, Saffi, or Azaffi, has rather an imposing effect, and appears to be nearly equal to Tangier in importance; but I was informed it is really very inferior to that place. It lies between two hills, and I believe is a locality of intense heat, and liable to inundations. The city of Morocco is about one hundred miles distant, in an E.S.E. direction. The vicinity of Saffi appears now to be barren and sandy, but previous to the erection of Mogadore it was the centre of European commerce, rendered so by its proximity to the richest province of the empire. It is said to have been founded by the Carthagenians. The inhabitants are chiefly Moors, estimated at about nine thousand.

Towards evening the weather became more unfavourable —I believe really stormy—and the idea of landing at Saffi was given up. Ferrache, who was unable to reach the ship, was left behind, to join us with the escort at Mogadore.

An accident occurred which might have been productive of serious consequences. I was awakened by a succession of claps of noise, so loud that, not being aware of our having departed from the port, I imagined that a nocturnal salute had been made, and it was not till the morning that I learnt that the connexion between the rudder and the tiller-wheel had been broken. A piece of the *iron lever* which connects the rudder with the ropes fell upon the captain's sofa at the stern, where our friend, Sampson Samuel, had been lying asleep a short time previously, having intended to pass the night there; but he providentially changed his mind and resumed his hammock.

MOGADORE.

Notwithstanding the darkness of the night, the mechanics on board succeeded, with considerable difficulty, in constructing a temporary apparatus by which the rudder might be effectually commanded; and a rough night being succeeded by a fine morning, we made the best of our way to Mogadore. Even there the landing, though better than at Saffi, is far from being safe or good. A trading vessel was a little before us, and its navigators, apparently well acquainted with the coast, boldly sailed to her anchorage, and led the way for the Magicienne. Soft bottom and a good anchorage was found; but these advantages do not appear to exist to any great extent.

The sea was comparatively smooth, but an extensive reef of sandstone rocks, lying between the port and Mogadore Island, renders landing dangerous to those who are not acquainted with the shore, as they are so much concealed at high water, that the safe channel cannot be distinguished. As the state of the weather was not to be depended upon, considerable exertions were made to hasten the landing of our effects. Captain Armytage undertook the charge of conveying Sir Moses on shore, and he was lowered in an arm-chair into one of the boats belonging to the ship, which was steered by one of our men who had been in this port before. Sampson Samuel and myself went in one of the boats of the country, which gave me an opportunity of witnessing the curious mode in which they are managed.

The boat, of rather rude construction, with high sides, more especially at its extremities, was piloted by an old man who was constantly shouting to the rowers with a loud voice. The men who rowed also shouted, and instead of sitting at their work, stood, alternately stepping upon the seat and throwing their weight upon the oar by leaning backwards, till obliged to step down to recover their balance. We took a circuitous course to avoid the rocks, and came to shore at an archway, under which the sea runs, where I easily managed to step from the boat, though it was evident that the assistance of porters must often be resorted to.

Amongst the first objects that caught my attention on landing were various old guns, of strange shapes and dimensions, and scarcely deserving the name of cannon. In appearance they were much like refracting telescopes, and reminded me of those that may be seen at the Castle of Wartzburg. We were conducted to the house of M. Corcos, who had, with great kindness and liberality, vacated it for our accommodation, and done much to provide for our comfort. Our large amount of baggage occupied the greater part of the inner court, as well as the apartments surrounding it. The town of Mogadore is walled, and divided into three compartments—the Christian, the Moorish, and the Jewish—having separate gates, which are closed at sunset. In the former, all the Consuls and Europeans reside. The streets are unpaved, and dirty in the extreme, more particularly in the Jewish quarter, where, huddled up in a small space, the filth in which the people live is indescribable.

The arrangements and packing having at last been completed, we started, amidst a crowd of spectators, chiefly Israelites, about two in the afternoon. Though the horses and mules, supplied by the government, were brought to our residence, we could not, all of us, find our respective conveyances. Sir Moses, instead of entering his vehicle, intended to mount the beautiful and well-saddled mule, lent him by M. Coreos; but finding it extremely difficult to get into the Moorish saddle, he, as well as Sampson Samuel and myself, proceeded on foot, till we had passed the walls. The vehicle intended for the accommodation of Sir Moses was a sort of wooden house or sedan, carried between two mules. The motion of such a conveyance is by no means pleasant; but it was easier for him than mounting horse or mule. We were accompanied by many pedestrians, besides a considerable number of persons variously mounted.

Amongst the latter were the Governor of the City, and other Moorish officers, the chief Israelite residents, both mercantile and Rabbinical. The Governor's party returned in about three quarters-of-an-hour, except most of the horse soldiers, who remained with us. Nearly all our Israelite friends accompanied us as far as our halting place, many of them having provided themselves with tents, bedding, and other necessaries. The French consul, his wife, and family, also rode with us during a considerable part of the way.

We passed the deserted palace on our right, and the long aqueduct, the Saint's Tomb, and the village Diabet on our left, and, ascending the hill, continued our course in a direction nearly coinciding with the coast, for more than an hour, and then, turning to the left, went more directly south. The first part of the way, the ground was altogether sandy and bare; but as we ascended the hill it became stony. The white broom, which was very abundant, scented the air with a fine odour; and liliaceous plants abounded, with some euphoria. Amongst the numerous loose stones, I saw many which were evidently fragments of stalactites, of great variety of size, some not larger than a finger, and others as big as one's leg or thigh; but they had little or nothing of a crystalline character. Trees of a species of olive, called argand, of a beautiful green colour, and producing a valuable oil, were increasingly numerous as we advanced, and of larger size. There were, likewise, other trees of a thorny species (lentiscus?). Though we still had sand, evidently blown inland, and encroaching on the productive tracts, we were sensibly coming on a limestone country, and the rock being almost bare, its surface was exposed, showing a large, flat, ramiform surface, in layers. Though not crystallized, it seemed to be of the same character as the travertin seen near Rome. Large portions appear to be undisturbed, at least unbroken, and in parts it lay on a slightly inclined plain.

Continuing our route through a woody country, and a little descending, we took a turn through an open space, on which hundreds of persons were collected, and there the work of unpacking the burdens of the loaded beasts, putting up tents, and cooking, commenced with much noise and confusion, as night was setting in, the various articles, and their uses, being imperfectly known. The Governor of the Province sent his brother, or brother-in-law, with several horse soldiers, to salute Sir Moses. They encamped near us. Ferrache knew the chief, having attended on him from the Red Sea to Morocco. A large mona or present was sent by the Governor, consisting of three or four sheep, many fowls, one thousand eggs, melons, a stupendous gourd, honey, ten pounds of loaf sugar, wax or composite candles, vegetables, &c. I retired to my solitary tent, which happened to be imperfectly closed, our men not having learnt how to put it up properly. A very heavy dew fell in the night; and between six and seven in the morning I rose, finding all my clothes excessively damp. The encampment, independently of the African peculiarities of camels, &c., looked very much like the site of a breaking up fair; tents in process of being taken down;

packing going on, and the ground well trodden and strewn with litters. Just as breakfast was announced, I was called to see an old relative of the Basha's brother, suffering from aggravated dyspepsia, senile debility, &c. After breakfast, the cavalry gave us a specimen of their galloping and shooting. Sometimes a dozen horse soldiers, dashing abreast, after galloping at a rapid pace for about two hundred yards, fired simultaneously at the ground, and then raising their long guns in the air, quickly stopped. We saw this sort of feat performed by an old officer singly.

The country which we passed through this second day was in many respects the same as that seen the day before; but the trees were finer and larger, and amongst them were common olives, as well as the argand. There was very little verdure between the trees. We saw several fields of corn, and ploughing with horned cattle and a rude plough. Our route crossed one or two extensive plains, the principal one traversed by a river, deeply sunk, having precipitous banks, showing the strata of alluvium, resting on the travertin.

We forded this stream, near the spot at which the party lunched, after having ridden about two hours and a half. The travertin was here exposed several feet in depth, and forming steps, composed of rounded pebbles, and a few shells, cemented by the travertin. There were many patches of a light, bright red, in the several layers of stone. This colour appeared to be derived from fragments of hematite, embedded in the rock. The pebbles are of considerable variety, many are of flint, schist, or calcedony, derived from veins or seams, as well as from nobules. There are also fragments of hematite, heavy and hard, yet susceptible of being scratched with a knife, and yielding a bright, red powder; and others of a silicious rock, apparently granular quartz.

In fording the river at this place, an accident occurred to one of the sumpter mules, which was carrying the baggage of our friend Chief Consul Reade. The animal had descended the steep bank, and fell, having missed its footing in the rugged and stony bed of the rapid stream, from which it was extricated with some difficulty, the baggage having become thoroughly soaked. A bridge might readily be constructed here; without it, the conveyance of baggage must be hazardous, and sometimes impracticable.

Loose fragments of the travertin, or tufa, are everywhere numerous, either thickly sprinkled over the plain or partially collected to facilitate cultivation. It would seem that layer after layer separate in fragments, which, from their structure, become easily broken. About an hour and a half after leaving the river we came to the bed of another stream, nearly or quite dry, forming a sort of ravine between low hills of limestone, the strata of which are generally inclined, with the stronger and thicker cropping out in ridges. At a little distance they so nearly resembled the layers of travertin, that I thought at one time there might be a gradual transition from the one to the other; but the path crossing one of these hills gave me the opportunity of seeing the travertin in a thin layer upon the broken edge of the older stone, like a carpet laid down upon a flight of steps.

The latter portion of the day's journey was by no means level, and we traversed thickets of white broom. Whilst crossing a high plain we had a beautiful view of the Atlas range, beyond the lower hills, which had previously bounded our horizon in that direction, that is to say, nearly south; the snowy peaks of the Atlas were apparently about three-fourths covered with snow, and were almost as fine as the Bernese Alps, seen from Berne. On our way we saw many wells and tanks, and, at a distance, several castellated buildings enclosed by walls, one, very large, in ruins. I also noticed single trees enclosed in walls, and was told they indicated Saints' tombs. About half-past four o'clock we came upon an extensive cultivated plain; we stopped for the night upon a sloping hill rising from it, but it was quite dark before the tents were pitched, and we dined very late. My wretched beast and worse saddle caused me to walk half this day's journey. The sky in the evening became overcast, and the wind rose so much during the night that fears were entertained that some of the tents might be blown down; they, however, stood well. Our men were very inexpert in putting them up, and as night closed before the work was done, some excuse must be made for them. Thanks to Captain Armytage, and our other friends from the Magicienne, our canvass lodgings were much improved by various corrections made by them; and mine, notwithstanding the wind, was really warm and comfortable. Sampson Samuel, who this night shared my tent, was by no means well; he had had a fall from his mule, and though he was not materially hurt his nerves were much shaken.

We all rose early on the 19th of first month, although we intended to make but a short journey. The spot on which we had encamped was situated a little above a large Saint's-house, which probably also served the purpose of a mosque. In its immediate vicinity a market is held on the third day of the week, and the place is known by an Arabic name which has this signification, Sidij-Mokhtar. In the immediate vicinity of the tomb are several small tenements and enclosures in rough stone work, apparently for the accommodation of market people and their cattle. A considerable number of persons had collected before we started, and I noticed baskets of corn and of various kinds of seeds, many pounds of honeycomb of a dark colour, sheep and goats tied together by the heads, horses, asses, &c. As we proceeded we met many of the country people coming by the path which we were taking, bringing their commodities to market. The country, however, appeared far from populous, but there were indications of its having had more inhabitants, such as ruins of large buildings, and extensive plots of ground which had at one time been cultivated. A number of wells and cisterns indicated a fair supply of water, but the absence of verdure in the large spaces between the trees was almost universal. We travelled for about two hours, in which we made satisfactory progress, and halted for an hour to lunch, and then continued our way over a very fair travelling ground, across a high, undulating plain, our course, though winding, taking a southern direction.

We had occasionally fine views of the long range of snowy mountains which we were perceptibly approaching, though they were still very distant. At first we had a country finely wooded with trees, mostly of the kinds before mentioned; many of large size. There were also patches of land, growing corn, some of which were enclosed with walls of uncemented stones, and others with dry thorny bushes, piled up to about the height of a man. Crocuses abounded the whole way from Mogador, and in this day's ride we saw many liliaceous plants of large size, and it seems probable that there is depth of soil to a great extent, though the prevailing character is still that of bare travertin, covered more or less thickly with stones, most of which are manifestly broken fragments, but others are a sort of boulder, having a nucleus covered with concentric layers, indicating the mode of formation, and it is remarkable that the nucleus is soft and pliable, like mortar, whilst the outward layers are compact and hard. Amongst the loose stones are silicious fragments, quite bare; a specimen of this kind was evidently part of a flint seam, with translucent parallel lines, and partially pink.

On some of the flat plots of ground which we passed near the camping place, the loose stones were small and of more uniform size, as if resulting from the breaking up of the travertin, where it has the character of conglomerate, as at the ford passed the preceding day. We continued our march much longer than we had expected, and Sir Moses did not finish his travelling until about half-past four o'clock, when he was much fatigued.

The encampment was near a good spring, with a pool containing small fish. Rushes abound in the neighbouring country. There was a pretty copse, as well as two or three palm trees, not far from the spring. Some of the party took their guns and went in quest of game, and Captain Armytage shot some snipes, which were dressed for supper, and proved delicious. Many partridges were seen, but they were too wild to be had. A bountiful mona was brought to us by the neighbouring chief.

On the high ground, above the encampment, are the remains of old buildings and walls rising but little above the surface; also an old cemetery, and a tomb, enclosed within rude stone walls. Within half-a-mile, in the same direction, are the remains of walls of large dimensions. The remaining scanty population cultivate the damp, low ground, and use cattle for ploughing, with a plough of rude form and workmanship. In wandering about I found numerous fragments of the nearly black volcanic stone, of which I had seen rarer examples the previous days.

At this halting-place we were met, on the evening of our arrival, by a courier who had come from Morocco to meet us. He travelled on foot, and though imperfectly recovered from a reducing illness of so severe a character that he had been quite laid up, he had performed the journey in about seventy hours. This man informed us that a little before he left the city of Morocco, a large government powder magazine had been blown up, and that not merely very extensive damage had been caused by the explosion, but six or eight hundred lives had been lost.

The night was cold, and Sir Moses suffered from it; we rose before seven o'clock, and started early. This day's journey of about nine miles, was chiefly over a nearly bare and almost level district, and we came near to the brink of a river of small size, and running in a bed with precipitous but not deep banks, through a loamy alluvium, which seems to be the residuum of a lake. Our road was for some distance over this soil, the surface still strewed with stones, and for a mile flint and chalcedony were so abundant that I dismounted, and in the course of a short walk picked up large masses of the latter, which seemed to be portions of meeting veins or isolated nodules.

A large one of the latter class had a cavity lined with milky botryoidal chalcedony. Masses are to be found bigger than a child's head, and apparently free from flaws. Such specimens might be worth collecting for the market, especially if susceptible of artificial colouring. These stones abounded for more than a mile, and then became much more scarce. The travertin still showed itself at short intervals.

Our route afterwards took us nearer to the mountain range which here bounded a considerable portion of the horizon ahead and to the right, but the snow seemed very much less general than at a distance it appeared two days before, when possibly a recent fall had produced a temporary covering. Some of the peaks were quite dark, and the sides, where bare, of the same shade.

We passed a few huts of the present poor inhabitants, and also low ruins of walls of great thickness, evidently the remains of a former period. It was thought by some of our party that they might be Roman, but I am inclined to believe them of much later date. I saw no mounds of rubbish, and few, if any, fragments of pottery, to indicate the existence of a numerous and long resident people.

Some persons from the huts stopped the cook and two companions of our fellow-traveller, Archibald Fairley, who were going in advance towards the halting place, and demanded money, showing a knife. The cook's party demurred, and were detained until his master, with his interpreter and soldier, came up. The soldier was called upon to do his duty. The man who had exhibited his knife denied the possession of one, but a large knife was found upon him, and the strong soldier gave him twenty heavy lashes, on the bare back, with a leather rope. The man afterwards kissed the knees of the soldier, and was led away by his people. This took place a little before we came to the spot.

We stopped for our resting place at a short distance from a well, with a small village on rising ground before us, consisting of walled enclosures for cattle, low tents for the people, and two poor mosques.

To the right, and in front, the snowy mountain range formed our horizon.

A small cliff of broken and bare stone, a little way from the camp, gave a view of a section, rather more than six feet thick, of the travertin, having much of the breccia character—the porphyretic, water-worn pebbles, chiefly of a green colour, indicating whence they were derived.

Our early halt gave us a good opportunity of looking about, and amongst the objects which we observed I may notice the following:—The well, before-mentioned, was very deep, and the people of the neighbourhood were pulling up their vessels with long cords which had worn the sides, as we may see in some of the marble mouths of wells in Italy. Here, however, the worn channels were not only numerous but deep, some being as much as four inches, which indicates great antiquity, for the stone—a buff and pink limestone, resembling Sicilian jasper—is very hard. The blocks themselves appeared to be portions of a stratum.

The people were very civil, and A. Fairley, having an interpreter, conversed with a Moorish woman, who invited him to her residence to take refreshment. He did not accept this kind offer, but subsequently went, with several of our party, including myself, to the village. We found it was objectionable for us to go into the large walled enclosures, the women of the chief being in one of them. We saw, however, that there were within very low brown tents, in which the different families resided. Besides the two mosques, conspicuous from a distance, there is a third, which has only the appearance of a rather high, but small, walled enclosure. The people whom we met were much interested in looking through our magnifying glasses and at our watches.

A chief and his servant rode up to us on horseback; the former held a French double-barrelled rifle, which he fired. There also came up to us a well-dressed person, evidently of superior rank, who, taking the chief's gun in his hand, went through various military movements, which some of my companions recognised as being of the French school. The same person came to our encampment in the evening, and presented Sir Moses with a handsome burnous, receiving, of course, a fully equivalent pecuniary present in return. The chief himself also came in the evening, and explained the reason of the smallness of his mona,—he said that he had been taken by surprise, and that his attempts to make a collection had been defeated by the poverty of the people. We noticed a plantation of prickly pear close to the village, and were told that the fruit was taken to market. It is a great pity that the people here do not cultivate this plant more extensively, and also introduce others, so as to raise more abundant provision for themselves and their animals. I noticed, near the village, a deep excavation, like a cistern, but it did not appear to be water tight, and probably served as a kind of cellar. The most remarkable point connected with it is the roof, formed of one large, thick slab of travertin, advantage apparently having been taken of making the excavation beneath it as it lay *in situ*.

After passing a comfortable night, we started about nine in the morning, resuming the road, from which we had a little deviated for the purpose of encampment, and proceeded towards the group of remarkably flat-topped conical hills, which we had beheld at a distance the preceding evening. Water-worn fragments of a green stone were seen in increased abundance amongst the loose stones strewed about. There were some patches of cultivated ground, but with the exception of scattered clumps of thorny shrubs, or small trees, which were not in leaf, the surface was generally bare, and to a great extent consisting of travertin. A small species of white snail adhered, in considerable numbers, upon the leafless boughs of many of the shrubs and trees, producing at a distance almost the effect of white blossoms. As we drew near the conical hills, the ground became thickly strewed with masses of flint and chalcedony. Some were of large size, many of them, when broken, exhibiting concentric lines, like agates, and varying in colour. When we had actually arrived among the hills, we found the ground whitened by their *débris*, consisting of fragments of nearly white limestone, resembling chalk, but harder — the silicious masses and nodules in profuse abundance, and varying in size from that of a hen's egg to more than a foot in diameter; in many instances they had somewhat of a stalactitic form, an unworn, but peculiar surface, rather mammilated than crystalline, and a fresh grey or mauve colour. We passed sufficiently near to some of these hills to observe that their flattened summits appeared to be occasioned by thickish beds of a silicious substance, resembling flint, chert, or jasper, lying parallel to each other, almost or quite horizontally. There were some smaller hills, from which it appeared that these beds had been removed, and their summits, instead of being flat, were rounded. When we were passing under one of the hills, we found the ground for some distance of a dark colour, from the abundance of fragments derived from the horizontal beds of flint; in many places the upper layers of travertin were still remaining, but in considerable tracts on the lower land, this had been removed, exposing the conglomerate bed, which, when mixed with alluvium, is available for cultivation. Some of these cultivated tracts appear to have been formerly lakes, or pools. It must be remarked, after we had passed the truncated, conical hills, we ceased to find any of the chalcedonic masses, though the water-worn fragments of green and other-coloured porphyry were very abundant, both loose and in the conglomerate beds, as well as in the beds of streams. Much of the latter part of this day's ride was over a merely flat plain, with very little vegetation, excepting the trees and shrubs already noticed, and some sprinkling of the white broom. We left the last of the conical hills a little to our left, and encamped by the side of a stream, in some places deep, flowing between fragile banks, consisting of the alluvium of the valley, resting on travertin. The bed of this stream is formed by water-worn porphyretic boulders. Oleanders flourish on the banks, the long seed vessels of which were bursting, and giving their downy seeds to the wind; these plants resemble our finest willow-herbs on a large scale. On the higher parts of the banks the white broom flourishes, and attains a large size. Advantage is taken of this water for the purposes of irrigation; a portion of which is drawn from the bed, and turned into an artificial channel, a little above, but nearly parallel to, the stream—as on some of our mill-streams—and it is probable that water power as well as irrigation might here be obtained. At some distance, and at a higher level, a long cliff exhibits a section of the travertin, showing the compact and comparatively pure upper portion, and the conglomerate character of the lower, which consists of green stone and porphyretic boulders and shingle, feebly cemented by the travertin limestone; a few similar water-worn stones occur in the upper portion.

Partridges and a few of the poules de Carthage were seen about our camp, and though they were very wild, some were obtained. A scanty mona was supplied at this place, and our vigilant companion, Chief-consul Reade, complained of it to the chief of the village, who was made a prisoner next morning; but he in his turn complained of one of his men, and gave him a beating. The last of the conical hills, which we had left, appeared to be so near to our encampment, that I greatly wished to visit and examine it, and as we had finished our day's ride rather early, there appeared to be sufficient time for my doing so; but my ever kind and anxious friend, Sir Moses, doubted the prudence of my re-crossing the stream and wandering so far from the encampment. I therefore abandoned the attempt.

We started early, soon after the contest with the chief whom we took along with us, and having gone about a mile we passed the left extremity of the conical mountain, the form of which is rather oval than circular. On viewing it from the other side, we not only saw the general direction of the strata—inclined somewhat from the horizontal—but had also the evidence of the wasting of the formation of which they are a part. Some of the smaller elevations, having lost their compact strata, at or near their summits, seem to be wasting, into the plain.

Our path lay between the remains of a strong and extensive walled fortress, within the remains of which is the residence of the offending chief, and a little modern village of mere huts, few in number. This, like other villages of the same description, is enclosed by a high pile of prickly bushes, in which is an opening for ingress and egress. It reminded me of the barricades which John Duncan describes the Amazons of the Gold Coast as being exercised in storming.

At the entrance of this, as of similar villages, I noticed some of the inhabitants sitting, as at the gates of ancient cities. Our way lay through a flat country, covered with alluvium of sand and loose stones, of the character last described, with travertin occasionally showing itself.

We did not intend to make a long journey this day, as Sir Moses wished to halt early to prepare for the sabbath.

Considerably before we reached the destined spot, we were met by a large, and, for the most part, superior company of Jews, well dressed, and mounted on good mules, who came from Morocco to meet Sir Moses, and pass the Sabbath in his company. They had left the city the day before, and recommended our halting near to the place of our meeting, and had induced our camel drivers, who preceded us with the tents, to stop, and pitching them had already commenced; but we persevered in our plan, and passing by the hills, leaving the nearest about a mile to our left, we encamped by a small stream of good water, used for irrigation in the cultivation of corn, prickly-pear, &c. Our tents were placed at the foot of a low hill, on the further side of it. It was one of a group of three or four to be described hereafter.

Not far from this place is a tower and a well-built walled enclosure, used as a caravanserie. Its construction is due to the benevolent and wealthy Moor, Emzodi, who effected many public works for the comfort and benefit of his countrymen.

Taking advantage of our early finish of the day's march, Dr. Forbes and I determined to retrace our steps and visit the nearest of the hills which we had passed; but, on our left, our attention was so much arrested by the interesting character of a smaller hill, or ridge, which we had not previously noticed, and which rises on the way we were taking, that we went no further. This ridge formed, in fact, a lower range; taking a direction parallel to that which we had proposed to examine, viz.: a little to the East of North and South. Our attention was diverted by finding loose angular fragments, which proved to be reddish porphyry and compact quartz, somewhat similarly coloured. As we ascended we found the same materials, but chiefly the latter, in large masses *in situ*. They formed layers of considerable thickness lying side by side, in the direction before-mentioned, and inclining a little to the West vertical, *i.e.*, towards the range to which we had intended going; they presented a bare, ragged, and angular surface, and the largest masses were so intersected with cracks that it would be difficult, or impossible to obtain a block of any considerable size, susceptible of being worked.

Though consisting chiefly of quartz, the layers were not of uniform character; some very closely resembled the petunse pentlandica; but the most remarkable layer, or bed, is one more shattered and easily disintegrated than the rest, in the course of which we noticed a pit surrounded with loose stones, and which had so artificial an appearance, that we supposed it to be so, and were at a loss to imagine its object. The approach of evening suspended our researches.

The next day, 23rd, I returned with A. Fairley, and in my way picked up a fragment of mineral, resembling, in colour and weight, magnetic iron ore, and we found that it sensibly affected the compass. My companion suspected that it was slag from a smelting furnace; but how could such a production come there? I had previously seen hornblende in a mineral; and my companion found another, in which I detected either hornblende, or small black crystals, which might be hornblende, but which resembled the black augite of Stromboli, except in being much smaller.

We went upon the hill which I had visited the previous evening, and confirmed the observation then made; but found the prevailing rock to be quartz, and compact felspar. No gold was seen in the former.

Tracing the particular layer, or bed, in which this pit was seen, it appeared possible that this hollow might be the result of a sort of land slip, down which water had run off, carrying all the small fragments, and leaving the larger masses. I descended into the pit, which was not deep, and found that it extended to a considerable distance, under so low a roof of rock, that no one could proceed in it, even creeping. I there found the *exuvia* of a good sized snake. Travertin still capped this formation even to a considerable height, but not at the top, where the numerous cracks in the hard, but shivered rock, promoted its separation, and brought to sight the renewed exposure of fresh surfaces. We proceeded to the nearest of the hills, rising to the West, which I had been unable to visit the day before. We had to cross a considerable valley, strewed with stones, in order to reach it, and then came upon quite a different formation. Though this range of hills was parallel to the smaller quartz ridge which we had left behind, and though the cleavages separating the rock into layers similarly sloped to the west, but inclining much further from the vertical, the character of the rock, which was not uniform throughout, was strongly marked by differences, taking quite a transverse direction, so that the side of the hill by which we ascended may not inaptly be compared to a page of a ruled book, raised to an angle of about thirty degrees—supposing the rock between some of the lines to be of marble, of a light, brownish colour, and coarsely crystalline, and between others a much darker and harder rock, sprinkled with small collections of a white crystalline substance. I could not determine what this substance was, but I found that, though hard, it could be scratched with a knife, and though not actually forming veins, it was deposited in the rock in short, curvilinear lines. The marble is in large, solid masses, intersected in different directions with real veins of a carbonate of lime, a little harder than the general mass, so as to cause a trifling elevation when exposed to the weather. The masses of marble presented, on the exposed surfaces, large broad slabs, not smooth and even, but having everywhere contiguous concave depressions of various sizes, which I may compare to the cast of a mammillated surface. This rendered it very easy and safe to walk up and down upon, notwithstanding the steep inclination, and the general breaking up into large masses. We noticed some curious, almost circular and vertical, hollows, in several of the beds of marble, the nature and mode of formation of which I cannot conjecture. A distinct covering of travertin, resting upon the marble, may be seen to a considerable height up this mountain range, but not at the summit.

The most remarkable discovery was made by A. Fairley, who, in looking about the marble beds, came upon the conclusive evidence of this stone having, at one time, been quarried for architectural purposes. Several large blocks were undetached, though the process of separation was considerably advanced; others, though detached, were so little removed from their original situation, that the corresponding marks of the tools might at once be seen on the separated surfaces.

The mode of working seems to have been very simple, and also very economical, both of material and of labour, and obviously consisted in making a channel in the direction of the intended cut, of the length required, and about three or four inches broad, but somewhat deeper, at the bottom of which holes were made, about three inches long, a little deeper than this, and scarcely an inch broad. The holes themselves might perhaps be four inches apart. My companion conjectured, with great probability, that wooden wedges were driven into these holes, and that water was poured into the groove above, by which the wood would be swollen till it caused the cleaving of the stone.

Besides several large blocks in the quarry, wholly detached, or very nearly finished, we found one piece, in the valley below, apparently designed for a column, ten feet long, with a proportionate diameter. This marble, though hard and sound, cannot, from its colour, be handsome; and I may here observe that I could nowhere find any specimens of it used, either in ancient or modern work, although I was sedulously on the look out for them during my stay in the country. I saw no indication of organic remains in this marble.

In the bottom of the same valley, the marble *in situ* was exposed over a large irregular space, with a flat, smooth surface, about three strides across, on which were some curious markings, not cut, but apparently made by numerous blows with a heavy blunt-pointed instrument. Though evidently designed to represent some objects, it is difficult to say what those objects were. These marks are probably of no long standing.

I much regretted that I was prevented visiting another hill of this ridge, though one general character seems to prevail throughout.

After my return to the encampment, I took an opportunity to examine some of the lower whitish-coloured elevations to the rear and sides of the camp. Even the highest is not so high as the porphyry or quartz range, and the others are much lower. The whiteness proceeds from the comparative purity of the travertin of which they are composed. It rests, however, on a bed of the travertin conglomerate, full of worn fragments of porphyry, chiefly green. Pebbles, or boulders, of the same character are thinly scattered through the more unmixed travertin. An excavation which has been made on the side of the hill, behind the camp, gave me the opportunity of ascertaining this with certainty. There was, beside, another peculiarity in this portion of the formation, which particularly arrested my attention. It has a strong tendency to disintegration, readily crumbling to pieces, part becoming a softish powder, which might easily be diffused through water for whitewash, whilst the other portion remains solid, in irregularly rounded nodules, from the size of horse beans upwards. Suspecting that they might be portions of some different and distinctly formed mineral, I broke several of them; but they seemed universally to consist of the travertin itself, very considerably indurated; and on carefully examining the fresh fracture of a good specimen, I noticed a multitude of minute specks, producing a greyish colour. They glistened a little; and as far as I could ascertain, with the help of a lens, on the spot, consist of minute granules of silex, deposited in very small cavities, such as would be left between concave surfaces, both concavities being turned the same way, and the larger curve being inwards. This instance, in addition to many others, of the deposit of silex in carbonate of lime formation, is worthy of notice. It does not seem to favour the animal origin of silex. Water freely filters through this travertin, and the stream in front of the encampment issues from pits, which have been sunk in it, about half a mile above.

With our accession of Israelite companions and soldiers, we formed a large troop, and intended this 24th day of 1st month, to take about half the remaining journey to Morocco. Our path to the city was an almost uninterrupted level, over a broad plain, between the lofty, snowy range on our right, and a lower, nearly parallel, range on our left, with an extraordinary number of conical summits, especially towards the East. Hills, of apparently distinct character, were scattered along their slopes, and a small, distinct cluster of seven summits lay between the two ranges in the distance, a little to the right of which we could just perceive the top of the lofty, ancient Kotabra Tower of Morocco. Before we had half completed the day's journey, we halted near to a deep well, from which the water was obviously drawn by means of a rope wound round a roller, resting upon two forked sticks, fixed on the wall. No rope or roller was there; but our active and efficient friend, Captain Armytage, presently provided a substitute, by joining together several pieces of the native cordage, which we had with us. When the water was drawn up, it was found to be cold, clear, and good in appearance, but with a very decided sulphurous odour, like that of St. Bernard's well, near Leith. This fact is not altogether without interest, in connection with the travertin formation. We saw but little of the travertin in this district; the upper strata had probably been removed, and the lower were covered with a deep, alluvial deposit, which might be fertile, though a comparatively small proportion is under cultivation. We passed several patches, on which ploughing was going on by different parties. The ploughs here are very rude, and they are drawn sometimes by two camels—sometimes by a camel, with a horse or an ass, or by cows or oxen.

Irrigation seems to be largely employed where cultivation is attempted. We passed several little streams, or beds of streams, having their course from the Atlas range, towards the river Tensift, which runs beneath the opposite range, but too far off to be seen.

We were here met by two of the Emperor's footmen-couriers who had been waiting some days for us. They were well-dressed, comely persons, well-built, and rather stout; and with their loose dresses did not appear exactly adapted for couriers.

It was our intention to encamp just beyond a larger stream, called the river Nefis, having the same course and destination as the smaller streams; but our camel drivers were disposed to bring us to a stop on an inferior spot, a mile short of it, and had commenced pitching tents there. We made them desist, and crossed the river, then of reduced size, though its stony bed, of considerable breadth, shows that it must often be larger. Threatening rain made it not improbable that it might be seriously increased before morning, and we were glad to ensure our passage. Rain fell during the night, and the morning was cool and damp.

Before starting on the 25th, I renewed the examination of the bed of the river, which I had commenced the preceding evening. It consists of pebbles and boulders of red, brown, and green porphyry, with some sprinkling of amygdaloid, quartz rock, and granite. The banks of the river are lined with oleanders. Ducks were observed flying about. The travertin bed was seen in section at one part of the bank. Where the banks were composed of dry, earthy alluvium, they were, in many places, whitened by a very thin, partial covering of an efflorescent salt, probably sub-carbonate of soda or natron.

The departure of our now large company from this encampment occupied a considerable time. The morning was gloomy, and a little rain fell. We still had the snow-clad Atlas range on our right, and the Jiblet hills bounding the plain to the left, the course of the river Nefis, which flows at the foot of the range, being distinctly marked by the trees which flourish on its banks.

MOROCCO.

As we approached within a few miles of Morocco, the lofty tower of Kotabra became increasingly conspicuous, and a few other towers of smaller size were visible, as well as a vast number of palm trees.

When within a few miles of the city we were met by about a dozen horsemen, remarkably well mounted, and, although not very richly dressed, wearing burnouses of a very superior quality, evidently indicative of rank; the trappings of their horses were in keeping. We were informed that they were all officers of distinction, sent expressly to pay their respects to Sir Moses. A halt of some minutes took place to exchange civilities. They then turned and accompanied us, though not very closely, but riding about, and giving us an opportunity of admiring their horses and horsemanship. As we drew still nearer to the city, we saw quite a crowd of its inhabitants poured out to meet us. Though they were chiefly Israelites, mounted on mules or asses, and who came out of respect to their distinguished benefactor and advocate, there were not wanting Moors, influenced by common curiosity. I was rather surprised to hear English spoken by some of the Israelites who came to welcome us. Here the palm trees were of large size, and in number they exceeded any that I had seen either in Egypt or Palestine. Very near the entrance to the town a low wall, with buttresses, external to the city wall, indicated the course of a considerable aqueduct, which, like the subterranean aqueducts, to be presently mentioned, serves to convey a good supply of water to the capital. A small rivulet, which is another means of irrigation, crosses the route to the city, and from some accidental circumstance Sir Moses narrowly escaped being overturned into it. We crossed a rather good bridge, about twenty-five feet wide — or roadway, with twenty spans, of about twenty feet each — crossing the river; this is a very old piece of work, but not at all a bad job, and is very strong, the piers being narrow and sharply pointed. From this bridge into Morocco, the road is exceedingly pleasant, as on either side there are nothing but gardens, with numerous palm trees—the date palm—all of which were heavily laden with fruit; there were also a number of little streams of water, which made everything nice and green, and which bore a striking contrast to the road, or rather track, before us.

Passing the city walls by a small gate we saw before us a loftier wall, with a large ornamented Moorish gateway, which, even in its dilapidated state, had an imposing appearance, and must have been magnificent when perfect. We afterwards learnt it was the entrance to the citadel as well as to one of the densest parts of the town. Between the two walls just mentioned is a large oblong arena, which is not merely a considerable thoroughfare, but is also a grand resort for horse soldiers, who spend hours there in that display of galloping and firing which, by English travellers, is called " powder play."

Having passed the gate of the first, or lower wall, we turned to our left, and came to a smaller door, which opened into a large but much neglected garden, well stocked with trees, some of which are quite old. Amongst these are orange and sweet lemon trees, with plenty of fruit. The sweet lemons, which I do not remember to have seen till I came into this country, are not unpleasant, but rather insipid, having less either of sweetness or of acidity than a good orange. Nearly in the middle of the garden stands the isolated quadrangular house or palace appointed for Sir Moses' reception. It consists of two stories, with an imperfect third. In the basement is an inner court, with a small fount in the middle, surrounded by apartments, which served as day-rooms, eating-rooms, and bed rooms for many of our attendants, as well as for kitchen and store rooms. The court is not open to the sky, as is common in Moorish houses, and its roof forms the floor to the court of the story above. A narrow staircase near the entrance leads to the next story, consisting of a larger and smaller hall, both of which are open to the sky, and partially surrounded by apartments devoted to the personal service of Sir Moses Montefiore, and also of his official attendants. From this floor another staircase leads to the roof, which is surrounded by a parapet. The openings to the halls below are similarly protected. Two small rooms taken out of the apartments on one side form the partial third story.

The first impression we received on entering this imperial residence was not very pleasing. There was a degree of dampness with a close and musty odour, which convinced us that it had not been recently tenanted; but a little observation sufficed to show us that it had been diligently put into something like order, and beautified, though still very deficient in furniture, and most of those things we regard as comforts; but there was a good deal of finery and effect in inferior workmanship. For example, there were pilasters and arches in plaster, and the capitals of the latter picked out in coloured wash. Paint, and white and yellow washes had been employed within and without. New Brussels carpets had been laid down on some of the floors; beds and ornamental pillows, either placed on European bedsteads, or immediately on the floor, were prepared in the sleeping apartments. Tumblers of cut-glass, gilt, for use at dinner; large earthen jars, capable of holding nearly twenty gallons, stood in the halls; but tables, chairs, and other seats were nearly, if not altogether absent. The windows were not glazed; but they might be closed by jalousies, or shutters, which, though they would serve to keep out light and rain, were ineffectual defences against the cold, which, owing to the proximity of the snowy Atlas range, made the nights of so low a temperature that we stood in more need of warm clothing in that part of the twenty-four hours than I have almost ever done in England. There were no fire-places, so we used the kitchen chafing dishes to give us a little warmth in the evening.

In the course of our ride from the river Nefis to Morocco, our attention was arrested by the subterranean aqueducts, which are a remarkable characteristic of this part of the country. Various series of mounds of earth, having nearly the same general direction, transversely across our route, were indications of the corresponding pits, from which the earth had been thrown out, to the depth of several feet. The bottoms of these pits communicated with each other, by lateral shafts, such as have lately been employed in laying down pipes, or making sewers along some of the roads, in the vicinity of London. In the channels thus formed, an abundant supply of water is conveyed from the mountain district, not only to the city, but also to the fields, and to the olive and orange orchards.

Several of these aqueducts were made at the expense of a benevolent and wealthy Moor, who has a strong claim upon the grateful recollection of his countrymen, not merely for these supplies of an article most necessary in this part of the world, but also for a large extent of garden ground, devoted to the inhabitants of Morocco, within their walls, and likewise for tanks and caravanseries, for the benefit of travellers. Much as these aqueducts are worthy of admiration, for the ingenuity and industry exercised in their construction, there are some serious objections to be urged against them. They entail an enormous and an incalculable amount of waste of water, by transmitting it through needlessly large channels, perforated through a porous stratum, namely, that beneath a continuous and more solid upper layer of travertin. Moreover, the sides of the pits being in no way protected, the loose earth and stones must be very liable to fall in, especially where the neighbouring population resort to them to fill their pitchers, by letting them down and drawing them up by cordage, without the aid of a windlass.

Immediately before entering the city, a long, well-constructed aqueduct, rising but a few feet above the surface, is one of the most striking objects which arrests the stranger's attention. I had no opportunity of seeing what means had been employed to form the channel from which the water flowed; but, within the walls, pipes, as well as open channels, are used, not only for gardens, and household purposes, but for ornamental fountains, of which we had a specimen in the grounds of the small palace assigned to us.

It can hardly be expected of a traveller who has visited Morocco that he has not paid some attention to the horses of a country of which the race is so remarkable. If the horses of Arabia have the most poetical and world-wide celebrity, those of the North of Africa—of which the horses of Morocco are the best—are scarcely less esteemed amongst connoisseurs. But of all the Barbary, or North African horses, those of Morocco have the most tried and acknowledged reputation, Morocco barbs being the ancestors of the best horses of which England can boast. In Tangier, where I saw chiefly camels, mules, and donkeys, I had but little opportunity of inspecting the horses; yet I saw a few examples, well-bred, and it appeared that they possessed much more bony strength in proportion to height than the generality of high-bred horses in England. I was informed that one of these was quite capable of carrying twelve stones, and proved himself able to do as much as a mile in two minutes. The horses at Mogador seemed to be of a very useful description, suited to heavy draught work, or more active service with the saddle, or in harness. I was not, however, particularly pleased with one or two specimens selected by English residents; which having slender limbs and elegant figures, and valued at a high price, did not appear to be likely to possess the qualities calculated to improve or sustain the character of English horses; and if such had been the Morocco barbs of late years imported into this country, it is by no means surprising that they have failed to support the reputation of some of their predecessors. In our journeys to and from Morocco, as well as during our residence there, we had opportunities of seeing horses, probably brought from different parts of the country, for the service of the horse soldiers and officers, as well as for that of the Sultan himself. Though differing considerably in size and colour, and somewhat in shape also, they had generally more or less of the figure regarded as characteristic of the barb, such as a good crest, and good hind quarters, with a somewhat declining croup, and large and low hocks. Some parts of the country enjoy a distinguished celebrity for their breed of horses, and if we may judge by the specimens in the stud of the Basha of Ducala, this distinction is not unmerited, for they certainly seem to combine points essential both for strength and speed. The Sultans of Morocco have been careful to maintain a stock of fine horses, and the splendid animal on which the present Sultan was mounted when he came in state to receive Sir Moses Montefiore, was one of a race which we were told had been for some hundreds of years in his family.

It cannot, however, be said that the Moors deserve commendation or imitation in the general management of their horses. I had no opportunity of learning how they fared when in the hands of their rearers, but when brought into service they are, as already stated, kept in walled enclosures, without shelter or litter, and so tethered by both fore legs by a rope passing round the pasterns, as not only to impede their movements, but also expose them to risk of injury. I never saw them fed with anything but beaten straw and barley, and the latter was given to the horses in our service upon the bare ground, whence it could not be eaten without danger of considerable mixture of the soil on which it lay. Though some of the animals had good coats for the time of year, I do not know that any attention is paid to grooming them; but it seems to be a common practice to lead them out to the exercising ground, or some other open space, where there might be a sufficiently large extent, sandy and free from stones, on which the animal was allowed to enjoy the liberty of rolling himself, which he continued to do with much agility for a considerable time.

The shoeing is, perhaps, the most remarkable, as well as the worst, employed in any country, where iron is nailed to the horse's foot, without any protection, as I noticed on my arrival in Tangier. The foot is almost wholly prepared for the iron by means of an adze, the butteris and the drawing knife, though not unknown, being very little used. The toe is abruptly shortened by a vertical cut, straight across the forepart of the foot, and apparently going quite into the quick. The nails are necessarily almost exclusively driven into the crust or wall; and as the frog is so pared as to remove nearly all that projects, the iron is continued across the heels, and turned up some way behind them. It is obvious that a shoe so applied must prevent all expansion. The feet are, consequently, narrow and contracted, and, but for the extravagant cutting of the toe, would become greatly elongated in that direction. Notwithstanding this, to my great surprise, I did not see the shortened step and unsightly crippled motion, so conspicuous in English horses having contracted feet. I can only account for this, that the practice of driving the nails in the French fashion, so as to come out not far above the shoe, relieves the soft parts within from the danger of pressure, occasioned by the presence of the nail to the length of time which the shoes are allowed to remain, as in the East, without removal; and also to the character of the ground over which they travel, which does not occasion the concussion, to which horses which travel on our harder roads are exposed.

Veterinary surgery in Morocco is, certainly, not superior to the art exhibited in shoeing. Amongst the wretched beasts which appeared to be emaciated by disease, I was particularly shocked by one which I saw under treatment. The poor creature was not confined in a travis; but a twitch, applied to the nose, was I think all that was employed to prevent his resistance. His mouth was bleeding from an operation which had just been performed for a well-known affection which impedes mastication, and this may probably account for the leanness of the beast. Actual cautery is the favourite remedy, and I suppose that this was thought necessary for the relief of some internal malady, for the old veterinarian, taking up a fold of the skin with his shoeing pincers, transfixed it with a hot iron pin, of about the size of a goose quill, and repeated the process on the different parts of the body and limbs.

The poultry of Morocco forms a very important part of the animal food of the country; we had as many as forty fowls given at one time in a mona, chiefly consisting of a small breed of game fowl. Their pugnacity is said to make them troublesome when collected for sale, or transport. When they are to be taken to any considerable distance, as from Tangier to the Gibraltar market, they are put into peculiar kinds of cages formed of large reeds, and made originally in a cylindrical form, but which become somewhat flattened when placed on the side with the birds in them; when taken to a shorter distance, either to a local market, or for mona, they are merely tied together by the legs, and it is very surprising to see the patience with which this restraint is submitted to. Perhaps the fowls, like the horses, are accustomed to this discipline, for I noticed some so secured in private dwellings at Mogador. The eggs in Morocco, like those in Egypt, are very small, even disproportionately so to the size of the chicken. As so prevailing a character must have a special cause, I have conjectured that it may arise from the hens having but a small amount both of water and succulent food. Turkeys, ducks, and pigeons are also used; but the two former bear a very small proportion to the chicken. The wild fowl are not abundant. My companions shot several very large and well-fed partridges, especially in the neighbourhood of Mogador; also different species of plover, snipes, and a few of a small species of bustard, strong on the wing, but short, though not deficient of strength in the legs. These are sometimes called poules de Carthage.

I noticed packages of ostrich feathers in the store rooms of our friend Corcos, at Mogador; but we did not see a single specimen of the living bird, nor any ostrich eggs, though they are much esteemed for the table, and serve as presents. Storks are not numerous; but, as elsewhere, they show no disposition to shun the abode of man, and are exposed to no injury, being regarded with affection, if not with reverence. In the city of Morocco I noticed their large and untidy nests, constructed of sticks, on a mosque, and on the walls about the citadel. There is another remarkable bird, which, in Morocco, receives equal esteem and protection with the stork; it is called by a name which signifies the cow-bird. It is of a milk-white colour, is rather larger than the largest crow, and has a large, light yellow coloured beak, and small eyes; it is a quiet and gregarious bird; I have seen nine of them on the upper branches of a tree in the garden, and not far from the house in which we resided. Though not an aquatic fowl it frequents the water sides, and I observed some of them about the large pools in the Sultan's garden, where I also noticed ducks and heron. Ravens are numerous, both near the sea-shore, and inland. They are of large size, and their plumage is beautiful. They do not seem to be shy, and in their flight approach so near to man that, not merely their hoarse voices, but the sound of their wings can be distinctly heard. They, doubtless, find an abundant supply of food in the carcases of camels, horses, and other large animals, which are left exposed, and are preyed upon by these birds, as well as by the dogs. Sparrows are seen, in every respect like those so common with us both in town and country; but they are not so numerous, or so bold as a very pretty little bird of about the same size, the greyish colour of which has a tinge of pale blue. These birds are very tame and bold, and come, with great freedom, into the apartments in quest of crumbs, which they pick up from the floor, and even from the table.

Our confinement to the premises which we occupied, and our consequent inability to see more than a little of the city and its vicinity until later, occasioned by the Sultan having deferred seeing us, was quite a trial. Some of our marine friends did not feel themselves so restricted, and took rides and walks, bringing home very poor reports. Sir Moses, Sampson Samuel, and myself strictly obeyed orders; but I made three exceptions to the rule of confinement, without disobedience. The Prime Minister had heard that there were two medical men in the party, and he sent word by our companion, the Consul, who visited him on business, that he wished to see us; but we were to go after sunset. We attended to his request, and, of course, could see but little of the town. His house is, I imagine, one of the few comfortable ones in it. We found it clean, and furnished partly with European, and partly with Moorish, articles. In a day or two Dr. Forbes and I repeated our visit, with a code of instructions translated for us into Arabic. The Minister then wished us to see a friend of his, and the following afternoon was fixed for our doing so; but when the messenger and mules came for us, I only was at home. My interpreter and I were conducted, as much as could be well managed, outside the town, but to save time, as the Jewish Sabbath was about to commence, and my interpreter being an Israelite, we returned by a shorter route, seeing more of the city. It is dirty, but large, and consists chiefly of thick and high walls, made of beaten earth, and enclosing spaces nearly vacant, in which are sometimes gardens, at others ruined houses, neglected ground, tanning pits, &c. The city walls are of the same character, but higher and thicker, with bad brickwork in places. The bricks are of old Roman character, but that which answers the place of mortar occupied more space than the bricks. Outside the walls are vast mounds of rubbish, the accumulation of ruins, refuse, and filth of all descriptions, probably of ages in formation. These banks of *débris* are resorted to largely by the Government for the preparation of saltpetre for gunpowder, and by poor people for their gardens. They also supply food to a little animal like a rat, but possibly a kind of jerboa, and to birds, and even dogs; for the carcases and bones of camels, horses, mules, and donkeys are scattered about amongst these heaps. There are also innumerable pits, some of great depth, which go down to water, and may be used by some to obtain water, and others to get rid of it.

On the 31st day we were informed that the Sultan could see us at half-past seven o'clock the next morning, and we had to be stirring early to be ready to keep his appointment. In the morning of the 1st day, February, the Prime Minister and the Chamberlain came to us. The latter was very solicitous that we should make haste and keep our time. All our party went on horses or mules, except Sir Moses, who used the sedan chair which had been brought for his service. This, I believe, caused some delay. We had about half a mile to go to the imperial premises, for we did not go into, or even in sight of, the palace. We passed for a considerable distance between two straight and high walls, made of beaten earth, a peculiar Moorish mode of building, which is more durable than could be expected. This straight lane was lined on both sides with troops, who had a very strange appearance. In clothing and arms they have quitted the old Moorish style, and become a sort of degraded European army. In the first place the men were of various ages, sizes, and colour—some old, others only lads; some quite diminutive, others tall; some as fair as almost any German, others the darkest Negroes, with every intermediate shade. In general, those who are quite dark, yet not black, have not the typical Negro countenance and hair, but on the contrary rather sharp noses, moderate lips, and straight hair. Many of the heads are shaven, but even then some hair is left which shows its character. Few, if any, of the men had shoes or stockings, but some I believe had slippers. I do not know whether they had shirts or not, but their old cloth jackets were indiscriminately of red, blue, or green. The garments worn for trousers did not cover the legs. These troops had very much the appearance of prisoners clothed in left off soldiers' garments. Each held a musket in due form by his side, but some had bayonets, others not. Even the officers were but little better clad. This lane opened into a very large open space surrounded by a similar wall, which was lined with soldiers, in some places in single and others in double line. Their appearance was in many instances far better than those above described. They were all foot soldiers, except the body guard, who made a fine appearance in white. To the left of the oblong quadrangle, which we entered by one of the long sides, was an appended quadrangle, at three sides of which were piazas with arches, with an arched gateway at one corner, through which the Sultan or Emperor came to us, as we stood at or near the fourth side, which is quite open to the large space or exercising ground.

THE INTERVIEW.

THE Emperor was preceded by a few of his guards, leading fine horses with rich saddles and trappings, and was accompanied by some of his Ministers. His Vice-Chamberlain had previously met us to announce that he was coming. The Emperor was almost entirely enveloped in his loose garments of white and pale green. He rode a remarkably fine horse, of pure white, at least sixteen hands high, of a beautiful form, yet very strong—an admirable model for an equestrian statue. The animal seemed gay, yet docile and good tempered, rearing several times while our interview lasted which did not in the least disturb his rider, who had possibly promoted it, though he looked very grave the whole time. The Sultan said he was pleased to see us as subjects of the Queen of England, that the friendship between England and Morocco was of long standing, and had been strengthened of late.

Repeating his desire to promote this friendship, Sir Moses said that he came in the name of his co-religionists and of the English people, and presented his address, which had been translated into Arabic. This sealed document the Sultan handed to his Vice-Chamberlain, who stood near, and presently withdrew, riding gently to the further end of the large quadrangle, at which stands a sort of summer-house or pavilion. He was attended or rather followed by his four-wheel carriage, which I had not before observed. It was quite covered up in green cloth. It is rather fantastically hung and must be light. It was drawn by one small horse. Our interview was not a long one, but I understand that it was one of the grandest which the Emperor has given, and marked by tokens of his entire satisfaction, especially shown in his riding a white horse, of a peculiar stock, which has been kept select in the family for many generations. The Emperor has a trying impediment in his speech, which is slow, and constantly interrupted by a noise, compared by some to a bark; yet the simile is not accurate. He is of dark, not black, complexion, somewhat marked with small pox; his features not Negro, yet his under lip is large and rather hanging; forehead good. He is about forty-five years of age, and is said to be a mathematician.

On the 1st of second month, we witnessed a remarkable atmospheric phenomenon, which probably bore some resemblance to the red wind of the desert, although of a much less severe character. Having in the morning paid our early visit to the Emperor, we felt at liberty to go out, and accordingly took a ride through a part of the city. Returning in the afternoon, the sky became overcast and cloudy, not only threatening rain, but rain appeared to be falling at some distance before us, and the clouds let down their frothy foams, of considerable length, in a vertical direction, whilst to the south and the very zenith, the air was of a gloomy brownish colour, appearing like so much smoke, that it was supposed by some of the party to be caused by lime burning. One or more of our native attendants said it was a peculiar fog. As we proceeded, the darkness approaching us, and we riding towards it, we met a sensibly cold wind blowing in our faces, and charged with a distressing amount of fine dust. The direction of this blast seemed to change a little, coming from the west of south, or rather, it appeared that the laden air was coming in two bodies, nearly in contact, but one to the west of the other, with a short, comparatively clear space between them. This, however, may merely have depended on the difference in the district over which the blast was coming. As we entered the city, it was evident that its own filthy dust was raised about us, to the great annoyance of our eyes, and we could not help thinking that such dust must be a prolific source of opthalmia. On our return, it was our immediate care, with time and pains, to purify ourselves from it. But a few drops of rain fell where we were. This blast lasted about an hour. The evening was fair and cool.

We paid a second visit to the Sultan, for the purpose of taking our leave. The preparatory arrangements very much resembled those on the previous occasion. The Chamberlain came to our residence to escort us, and horses, mules, and guards were in readiness to conduct us. We entered the Sultan's quarter by the same gate, and proceeded along the same walled road, lined as before on each side by foot soldiers, till we came into the vast walled enclosure in which the Sultan had received us; but now, instead of his meeting us here, we were conducted to the opposite side of this Moorish Champ de Mars, through a gate, under the pavilion figured in the sketch, into an apartment of considerable size, which served not only as a passage to the garden, but on the left as a waiting room, and on the right as a kind of office for scribes, several of whom were engaged in writing—in the Arabic fashion—upon their knees, bent in the manner of our tailors. Here we remained some minutes, which gave us the opportunity of watching these Moorish clerks, as well as of seeing several of the Sultan's officers, of different grades and shades of colour, who appeared to be preparing for the ceremony in which we were to take a part. When the Sultan's readiness to receive us was announced, we proceeded, for some little distance, along the straight path of an extensive garden of orange, lemon, olive, and other trees, till we came to the large summer-house or pavilion. The Sultan was seated in the Eastern fashion, on a raised divan, in an alcove in the side of the building furthest from the door. He was dressed much in the same style as when we saw him on horseback. His manner was perfectly courteous, and, in a conversation of some length, in which our friends, Consul Read and Moses Nahum, acted as interpreters, he exhibited much less of that impediment to articulation, which had rendered his speech, on the former occasion, somewhat painful.

The pavilion in which the Emperor was seated was square, with a pyramidical roof. The floor, which was raised above the ground, and the walls within were covered with rich mosaic of minute glazed tiles, in which green predominated. The interior of the roof was also richly decorated. This was the only apartment into which we were admitted, having anything like imperial magnificence. When the interview was concluded, the Sultan ordered a considerable body of guards and other attendants to conduct us through the extensive grounds connected with the palace, but from which no view of the imperial residence could be obtained.

It is difficult to give an adequate description of these grounds, which, enclosed in high walls, seem to unite the character of garden, orchard, and field. Besides canals for irrigation, there were two large quadrangular pools, or lakes, of water, on one of which was the working model of a steam boat, but the paddles were turned like a grindstone, by the single navigator who was on board to exhibit it. This good supply of water, not only added to the fertility of the ground, but improved the view, which was enlivened by numerous wild fowl.

The orange, lemon, and other fruit trees were very abundant; but we were particularly struck with the number and superiority of the olive trees, which were then laden with ripe fruit of large size. The trees themselves were generally superior to almost any olive trees to be found elsewhere, having noble, healthy trunks and vigorous branches. A long, straight path, or road, of several feet in width, running through the principal olive yard, is covered with vines, trained over it, and supported by lattice work. This not merely serves to afford a most grateful shade, but must yield a very valuable crop of grapes. In fact, the Sultan derives no inconsiderable revenue from the produce of these grounds, which we were informed had been laid out by renegade Spaniards, who had adopted the Mahometan faith. We also understood that the annual produce is farmed by Israelites. In the grounds we noticed a building of considerable size, undergoing repair and addition, but we did not learn whether it was designed for a dwelling or merely to be used in connexion with the produce of the grounds. The building material, as usual, was rammed earth, or tappia.

Though we made our visit mounted, and Sir Moses in his sedan, and lingered nowhere, our survey must have occupied hours, which will give some idea of the extent of these grounds, which are really worthy of a Sultan's domain.

It was intended that we should have visited the grounds on an earlier day, but at the time proposed it happened that the Sultan was amusing himself in the gardens with his children, which set aside the arrangement; but it had at least the advantage of giving us this little insight into the character of the Sultan as a family man.

After leaving the Sultan's domains, we proceeded to the Jewish quarter, which, though poor, was not materially worse than other parts of the city. It appeared to be densely inhabited, but our visit did not furnish a fair opportunity of judging of its character in this respect, as the whole

Israelitish population seemed poured forth to gratify their curiosity, as well as to do honour to their almost adored friend. The streets, or rather lanes, being narrow, it was extremely difficult to move through the crowd, although the Sultan's guards, and some of the Israelites themselves, used great exertions, and even employed blows, to clear the way. Sir Moses's sedan could scarcely be carried forward, and his companions, for a considerable part of the way, found it necessary to go on foot, and I believe, like several in the crowd, were not always able to keep on their legs.

Sir Moses, as usual, first visited the synagogue, or rather one of the synagogues. It was a small, rudely decorated room, with evident indications of antiquity; but had the raised reading desk, and other requisites of Jewish worship. The crowd was so dense that it was with difficulty we entered. This was the only occasion of my visiting it, and I regret my inability more completely to examine and describe it. We did not enter any of the other synagogues, having visits to pay. Sir Moses called upon some of the rabbis, where, from the pressure of the crowd, it was impossible for us all to follow him; but we were more successful in gaining admission to the house of M. Corcos—perhaps the wealthiest of the resident Israelites—who had not merely met us on our way to Morocco, but had been assiduous in his attentions during our stay there. His house, though in a narrow lane, was of good size, as usual surrounding an inner court, and two, if not three, stories in height. We were assembled in the court, where members of the family, richly dressed, received us, and supplied us with tea in the Morocco style, and with abundance of sweet cakes. Whilst we were so engaged we were gazed upon from the upper windows by many well-dressed Jewish ladies; but it is probable that they were not all members of the family. The vessels were of glass, gilt, served upon chased brass salvers, such as we had seen manufactured at Mogador.

We likewise visited M. Nahum, who had been equally kind and obliging with his neighbour. His dwelling was of the same style, and I may briefly observe that, though the streets were narrow, and not well kept, the dwellings we entered generally appeared cleaner, and in better order than might be expected.

On second day morning, the 8th of second month (February), we started from Morocco on our way to Mazagan. Although we had now become accustomed to the mode of travelling we were about to adopt, and the preparation for starting was therefore not so difficult as when we were leaving Mogador, there was nevertheless much to be done.—Sir Moses had numerous parties to take leave of; Dr. Forbes and myself had still many patients to attend to, and many more were necessarily left without relief, from the want of time, and from deficiency of the means required to assist them.

It had been arranged that we should use mules only, giving up camels for the tents and baggage, and horses for riding, with the single exception of our friend, Consul Reade, who, like the soldiers that escorted us, preferred horseback, and kept the excellent little animal which had carried him from Mogador. We had also with us a fine young horse which the Consul had bought, but he was led the whole way. The active and efficient officer who appeared to be the second in authority in our journey from Mogador, now became the chief, and he was accompanied by some very civil, well-appointed horse soldiers.

The chief took with him his servant, mounted on a baggage mule, and a poor little lad, who, if he had not a considerable amount of negro blood, was a very dark Riffian. Like many of the poorer class to which he belonged he was nearly blind of one eye, having suffered from chronic opthalmia. He excited our commiseration, for, though good tempered and obliging, we thought he appeared hardly treated by the overbearing and selfish servant of the chief. When with some difficulty we were at last all in motion, we found the streets and lanes thronged with people to witness our departure, or to accompany us on our way: many, if not the majority, were Israelites, and not a few continued to press around their benefactor, seeking further gifts in addition to the bountiful distributions which he had bestowed. The encumbrance and impediments which this occasioned called forth several exhibitions of a kind of corporeal punishment, employed by the Moorish police, and in a few instances I saw it applied by our own soldiers, and even by Israelite hands of the higher class.

Taking our course towards the Jiblet Hills, our road at first was the same as that by which Captain Armytage started for Saffi; but we afterwards turned off a little to the right. Had it been prudent for me to allow our party to proceed without me I might, even at this late period, have had an interview with the Maltese savant, as he sent me an invitation by the Israelite engaged in the saltpetre works, who kindly undertook to conduct me to him. Solicitous as I was to become acquainted with this well-informed citizen of Morocco, I did not feel justified to make the attempt.

We had not at first taken the usual path to Mazagan, and were conducted across the partially cultivated country to the ford of the river Tensift, near which we came upon the direct road. On our way I noticed some granite millstones a yard or more in diameter, and evidently heavier than a camel could carry. I was informed that they had been quarried in a neighbouring hill, from which they were rolled to the city.

The use of granite in making millstones is, doubtless, the cause of the gritty character of the bread in Morocco.

T. F. Reade and myself were amongst the first to reach the ford. The river was extremely low, taking a very winding course through the valley, which, when it is full, forms its bed.

We waited on the further side for our companions to come up; and whilst I was engaged in attempting to make a sketch, a negligent and clumsy mule driver, who was riding one of the animals laden with tent apparatus, tilted at me with the poles, and though called upon to desist, persisted in doing so till my saddle turned round and I was thrown upon the ground. Before mounting I had noticed the slackness of the girth, and made the attendant alter it in my presence, though the result showed how inefficiently he obeyed, which might be owing to the absence of buckles, which are not used. My mule was not better than the saddle. Declining to mount again I performed a good part of the remaining day's journey on foot, which gave me an opportunity of quitting the path to examine objects by the way.

My attention was particularly arrested by what appeared at a distance, about a mile to the left, like new white buildings, or high blocks of quarried stone. On coming up to them I found that they were projecting portions of a vein or dyke of quartz rock, about sixteen feet across, and cropping out as far as my eye could trace it. Besides the enormous blocks which were seen from a distance, innumerable fragments strewed the neighbouring ground, which was whitened by them. The surface generally might be described as an inclined plain, sloping towards the hills we were approaching. The rock which this and other quartz veins traversed was schist of different colours. Although this rock was extensively laid bare, we frequently observed the travertin lying upon it.

We did not travel more than about fourteen miles and a half this day, making our encampment at Boo Limoor beside a small rivulet, where were a few native dwellings, near which some of the most picturesque of the Jiblet Hills arose to sight. There were trees and cultivated grounds in the vicinity of the stream; but at a short distance the rock was generally loose quartz, protruding in massive dykes, the fragments of which whitened the ground, strikingly contrasting with the schist, the layers of which were so nearly vertical that their edges often formed the surface.

On the morning of the 9th, shortly after starting, we commenced the pass of the Jiblet Hills, which are here composed almost wholly of schist with veins of quartz, which, from its decomposing character, is, in many places, strewed over the ground. The path was seldom inconveniently steep, and was sufficiently worn to be tolerably easy for travellers on foot and on horseback; but the projecting ridges of slate made it very uncomfortable both to Sir Moses Montefiore and Sampson Samuel, whose vehicles, slung between mules, were constantly liable to be brought into collison with these unyielding obstacles.

The opening between the hills was sufficiently wide to afford a fine view of the snow-covered Atlas range, and the extended plain which lay at its feet between us. On our route this day an incident occurred which I think may be mentioned as a solitary one of Sir Moses Montefiore meeting with anything like a personal insult from a Moor. As I was riding a little in advance I was not a witness of the affair, but I was informed by T. F. Reade that a fanatical countryman came up to the side of Sir Moses' carriage and not only used insulting language, but actually spat into the carriage of our excellent friend. For this outrageous assault he was seized and taken along with us to our next encampment.

Schist was quite the prevailing rock, and it was generally so placed that its edges formed the surface; it was usually in thin flakes, and so broken by fissures that probably no part of it could be converted to use, besides which the flakes were far from presenting a flat or even appearance; this, however, was not the universal character, as T. F. Reade, who being well mounted could occasionally deviate some distance from the track, observed slate of a good quality, and well adapted for building purposes. Though we had reached the highest point, and commenced our descent before coming to our camping ground, we found the evening cold, and some fall of rain rendered it very uncomfortable. As we descended, the ground was slightly undulating, and on the sides of one of the little hills, which, being at no great distance from the road, I visited, there was a Moorish burial ground of considerable extent, in which the graves, that were thickly placed were marked by pieces of slate placed vertically at the head and foot; no workmanship appeared to have been bestowed upon them. I did not notice any habitations in the neighbourhood, therefore it would seem that either the population had diminished, or that the Moors are not averse to convey their dead to a considerable distance for interment.

Our halting place was called Sahrij, near to a large covered tank, built by the benevolent Moor, Emzody. Here we met several natives, some of whom appeared to be travellers like ourselves, and the water in the tank was so stirred up by their vessels that it was perfectly thick, and of a dirty reddish brown colour, and of no agreeable taste.

Doctor Forbes and myself endeavoured to extemporise a filter with a clean towel, made into a conical bag, partly filled with some of the beautifully white quartz pebbles which abounded on the ground, mixed with pounded charcoal; but, though we produced considerable improvement in the water, it was still unfit for use; whilst our friend Reade, who was provided with a composition charcoal filter, in combination with a flexible syphon, was not more successful; and after persevering in our attempt for a considerable time, we were obliged to put up with some water little better than that in the tank, which our cook obtained at a short distance. The ground in the vicinity of the tank appeared to be artificially sunk, so as to form a sort of basin, having a considerable area; but whether it was really artificial, and for any definite object, I did not learn.

Tenth of the second month.—The weather improved and became much milder. In the morning the prisoner who was taken the preceding day, received the punishment of a thrashing, and was permitted to depart, after having been told that our Consul would so far pass over the offence as to forbear making the complaint to the Moorish Government, which he would have been justified in doing. I saw the man striding away at full speed across the fields on his return home, and was not aware, until then, of what had occurred.

The land on the lower side of the Jiblet Hills is, probably, much higher than the plain between them and the Atlas range, and as we proceeded northward, we repeatedly obtained fine views of its snowy peaks over the summits of the intervening hills. The travertin, which was partially present, even on the Jiblet Hills, became much more prevalent, and considerably thicker, as we approached the undulating plain to the north-west. We saw to our right, but at a considerable distance, some conical hills, with flat tops, resembling those which we had passed near to Shishowa, on our way to Morocco; but those nearer to us and to our left, were much reduced in size, and of rounded outline. The ground which we traversed in this part of our route, was strewed with nodules and fragments of chalcedony, resembling those which we had seen in our outward journey. The travertin bed was thick, with an abundant conglomerate bed beneath it. Over tracts of considerable extent the upper layer of travertin was so continuous and undisturbed, as almost to pave the face of the country. We passed some true limestone, which protruded, in nearly horizontal beds, from the sides of the hills, and it was not always easy to distinguish them from the travertin, of which the layers were frequently thick and compact. It is a part of the country which seems to merit careful geological examination.

SMIRA.

Our halting place was at Smira, signifying sandy, where there are considerable remains of buildings, now in a state of ruin, though the tower of one of them, probably a caravansery, is still standing, and of considerable height. As we halted in good time in the afternoon, I took advantage of the opportunity to retrace our steps for a mile or two, and more closely examine the white chalk-like limestone of which the conical hills were composed, and which, for a considerable distance, was in close juxtaposition with the travertin and conglomerate bed. The examination was highly interesting; but as I have already described the appearances which we observed in a paper presented to the British Association, I need not repeat them here. Evening was drawing on when we returned to the encampment, and my companion noticed a specimen of a very small species of owl, which flew about at no great distance from us for a considerable time; but as he had only a small pocket pistol, his repeated attempts to shoot it were unsuccessful.

Several Moorish families have taken up their residence at Smira, attracted in part by the supply of water, brought apparently by a subterranean aqueduct to the neighbourhood, and probably in part also by the ruins, which appear to afford enclosures for the preservation of cattle and some of the dilapidated apartments seem also to be turned to account; but the people themselves are lodged close by, in the ordinary huts of the country. Excavations beneath the travertin here, as elsewhere, are used as a kind of cellar. Ravens were numerous, and the skeletons of animals, lying on the ground, are all that remain of the carrion by which they were attracted.

On our leaving Smira, on the 11th, we came, after riding a few miles up on a more open, level, and better-cultivated country, and were met by a company of horsemen, the military companions of the son of the Kaid Mahomet Ben Jelaz, sent by his father to press us to change our route, in order to take up our abode for the night at his father's residence. We were not aware of the amount of circuit which this deviation imposed upon us, and the invitation being urgent and cordial, Sir Moses consented to accept it. By doing so, we missed passing by a place, formerly occupied by the Portuguese, and where, we were informed, there are buildings erected by them, and several objects of interest still preserved. Although, after the first few miles, we were clear of hills, and the ground, generally level and extensively cultivated, was much more favourable to expeditious travelling, the distance was so great, that it was already approaching dusk when we halted, and on no day did Sir Moses appear so completely fatigued. We were not admitted into the Kaid's residence, or within its walled enclosure, but we received a bountiful mona, and a supply of ready-dressed provisions, served up in a manner very much resembling that which we had seen before in the salon of the Oozier, at Morocco. One of the dishes was peculiar. It consisted of a kind of broth, or thin stew, prepared with goat's meat and some farinaceous matter, esteemed amongst the Mahometans, and used to break their fast in the evening during the Ramadan. This, like some of the other dishes, was not generally partaken of by our party; but I tasted some of it, and found it by no means unpleasant.

From what I was able to perceive of this Kaid's residence

from above his walls, and from indications of his mode of living and possessions, he must be in a much more affluent position than his countrymen; but I heard it conjectured that he might not be in perfect ease and safety, and that his extra attention and politeness to us might, possibly, have an interested motive, as the means of securing the favour of the Sultan. Be this as it may, the province of Ducala, in which he resides, is one of the most productive in the empire of Morocco. Even here the population is scanty, but it is due to them to observe, that nothing bordering on insult or rudeness was shown to us. On the contrary, they treated us with politeness, and, in some places, brought us good new milk, which proved very refreshing.

The next day the morning was fine, and we continued our journey through the province of Ducala; cultivation is rather general, and the unploughed land was rendered verdant by the abundance of liliaceous plants, many of them coming into flower; palmetto is abundant, and the prickly pear, which grows to a great height, is used for fencing. We passed several villages. The wells, which are numerous, are deep; and having an opportunity of examining the earth excavated from one of them it appeared to consist of unusually sandy travertin, in which were some crystals of dog-tooth spar, and some rather equivocal traces of shells.

During this day's ride we still occasionally caught a glimpse of the snowy tops of the Atlas range, which we had now left far behind us. In the afternoon we drew towards the citadel, or large walled enclosure of the Basha of Ducala, which, as we descended along a slightly inclined plain, was seen for a considerable time before we reached it. This Basha is a wealthy and powerful prince, and was the most hospitable and generous provider amongst those whose attention we received in the course of our Morocco travelling,

not even excepting the munificent prince who greeted us on our first encampment on leaving Mogador. The Basha of Ducala not only received us within his walled enclosure, but into his private premises, though not into his residence; but his garden, in which were two or three pavilions, was allotted to us; the largest pavilion, which was enclosed, formed a very good apartment for Sir Moses, whilst three of the tents were pitched for some others of the party. In this garden, besides orange and other fruit trees, cotton had been cultivated, and I saw a few dried remnants of last year's crop. There is a large well in the garden, from which the water is drawn by means of earthen pitchers, worked by a wheel turned by beasts, as in Syria, but it was not in use at the time of our visit.

The following day we rested, it being Sir Moses' Sabbath; our time, however, was fully employed. The space occupied by the enclosing walls is large enough for the site of the town and the population, besides the Basha's own attendants, who are numerous. In one large open space, answering, in some respects, to the *grand place* of a French town, our horses, mules, numerous retinue, camping apparatus, and other baggage were collected; and here, it would seem, that travellers and their beasts seek rest. Those who may be regarded as habitual residents seem to live in tents, a few of which are pitched without the walls, but the majority are within them.

The Basha insisted upon presenting Sir Moses with a horse, and desired he would take his choice from the entire stud. For this purpose T. M. Reade and myself made repeated visits to the Basha's fonda, a large uncovered enclosure, in which many fine horses were tethered by the fore feet, yet not so closely as to prevent their lying down upon the bare ground when they inclined to do so. The horses of this province are greatly esteemed, and those which we here saw were of large size, with strong, bony limbs and ample muscular development, yet their good breed was very evident, and it was not easy to take advantage of the Basha's generous offer, and decide which to choose. Two or three which had been placed in the Basha's stud by the Sultan himself were necessarily excluded from the number from which the selection was to be made; but they did not appear to possess any extraordinary merits to entitle them to claim much superiority over their companions.

A considerable number of Israelites reside in tents within the Basha's citadel, which being placed contiguous to each other form a quarter of their own. At the time of our visit the population of this quarter was, I believe, increased by the relatives or friends of the customary inhabitants, who had come from other parts to meet Sir Moses. A merchant of this class presented Sir Moses with a fine young horse, which much reminded me of Theobald's celebrated stud horse "Camel."

The fact of there being medical men in Sir Moses' company brought us several applicants for advice; but our store of medicines had been nearly exhausted before leaving Morocco, and the remnant was imperfectly accessible.

The night proved inclement, and so windy that the poles and pegs of our tents, being stuck into garden mould, threatened to lose their hold, and allow the canvass to fall upon us in our beds; but we happily lay till morning without experiencing any great adventure.

Before our departure the Basha, with his officers seated beside him in their white burnouses, received us in a small, open pavilion, looking not upon the private enclosure, but rather on a space accessible to the public, and, therefore, such as may be supposed to resemble a place in which, in ancient times, the principal men of the city might be seated at its gate. This Basha has been in office about twenty years.

He appears to be a fine character, and the number and good condition of those about him, speak much in his favour.

We started about nine in the morning and passed through a well-peopled district, in which were several chiefs' residences, in walled enclosures, besides huts and tents for the peasants. Where the ground admitted of it, cultivation was general; but there was much travertin, either bare, or thinly covered with silicious sand and with reddish brown dust, mixed with vegetable mould. The character of the country was undulating, producing a succession of flattish valleys, with limited horizon. Wells are frequent and deep. We saw several small cisterns, made by taking advantage of the shape of the travertin rocks, which were so disposed as to form convex elevations; these, when properly cut off and turned over, furnish good sized basons.

We came to our encampment in an open country, near a pool or well, with rising ground both before and behind us. At this spot we were joined by a party of Israelites, who came across the country to our right, in order to pay their respects to Sir Moses.

On the second day we started with a fine morning, and travelled over a tract of country similar to that which we had passed the preceding day, but abounding with detached pieces of travertin, many of which were very large. Much laborious industry is employed in collecting them to form uncemented walls, having some resemblance to those of Warwickshire, but of greater thickness. They are also formed into heaps, apparently for the purpose of clearing the ground.

We made our midday halt at a spot whence a little town, one hour and a half's ride from Mazagan, may be seen. In proceding from thence, we were met by the British Vice-Consul and several English and other European merchants, remarkably well mounted; and, almost simultaneously, Sir Moses was greeted by a very numerous and remarkable group of his admiring co-religionists. They did not seem disposed to form themselves into any particular order of march, even had the irregularities of the country allowed them to do so. A more varied or motley assemblage could scarcely be described or imagined. There were old and young, rich and poor, male and female, either going on foot, or mounted on horses, mules, or donkeys, with or without saddles, and in some instances two individuals on the same beast, whilst their costume was quite as varied; yet, perhaps, the garb sometimes forced upon them by the Moors predominated.

Amongst the crowd were several poor women, who carried, as substitutes for flags, handkerchiefs tied to reeds. The concourse swelled as we proceeded, and it did not move in silence, but on the contrary with much noise, especially that produced by the vibratory motion of the tongue, as expressive of joy.

Nearer to Mazagan the palmetto becomes abundant, and there is much increased natural vegetation, in great variety. We received intelligence of the "Magicienne" lying off the port, and of our friend, Captain Armytage's, anxiety to leave, he having recalled the officers, who had gone on shore to shoot. As we were entering the town we met several of these gentlemen, who greeted us with much cordiality.

The high ground near the coast prevented our seeing the town till we were almost upon it; but we caught a glimpse of the sea and of our ship. To the north of the town is a remarkable object, which may be either a rock or a ruin—the latter seemed the more probable.

Sir Moses' first object was to go to the synagogue, to arrive at which he had to pass through several streets, greatly crowded by persons of all ages, various ranks, and both sexes; and as we had dismounted before arriving at the synagogue, we entered it with difficulty, though we were cordially and energetically assisted to do so. The synagogue, rather a small but very neat upstairs room, was completely crowded, and the English Vice-Consul, and other visitors besides ourselves, added to the congregation.

A somewhat long service was performed, a considerable part of which consisted in the reading of a Hebrew composition, specially prepared by the Chief Rabbi for the occasion, and in which the names, not only of Sir Moses Montefiore, but of Queen Victoria were introduced. It was read by the Chief Rabbi, whose voice and mode of delivery I heard much praised.

From the synagogue we passed, without returning to the street, into the adjoining house, occupied by an Israelite, who had a well-furnished, good establishment, in character and style resembling those of the same class in Mogador. The mistress of the family, who was richly dressed, was quite an attractive person. From this house, where we did not stay long, we went some little distance, to the residence of another important Israelite, where provision had been carefully made for our refreshment and lodging. Here we were joined by Captain Armytage, who, the weather being favourable, was very anxious to hasten us away, and was earnest and pressing that we should at once go on board, and not lose the opportunity. So much, however, still remained to be done in settling with, and taking leave of, the large number of Morocco attendants who were going no further, that the idea of our getting away before the morning was quite out of the question. Indeed M. Mahon, with whom the charge of this arrangement chiefly rested, was engaged the whole night, and then, with much exertion, only completed the task after we were all on board.

We made a capital repast at a well-supplied table, at which

were good wines of several kinds, liberally supplied by our Vice-Consul, Octavus Stokes, who was very active as well as generous, in endeavouring to gratify and assist us. He was, besides, a very interesting person, and had travelled and seen much, having at one time resided in California.

His house, which he has capitally constructed and arranged out of a deserted Portuguese church, is probably the best in Mazagan, and from its tower the English flag is well displayed. He not merely invited me to his house, but very kindly wished to show me the interesting objects of the place, more especially mentioning a large and remarkable reservoir for water, constructed by the Portuguese. Though I managed to see his house, I had no opportunity for doing more. There was no time or daylight in the evening, and in the morning we were hastened away at an early hour. On the route to the pier, I saw various evidences of the activity of the port and of the amount of business carried on by a few native and European merchants, the former being chiefly Israelites. A good stone city wall rises at the sea-side, and some few yards from this, and parallel to it, is a stone pier of considerable length, which forms a long basin or dock, which must be of great service for the lighters, or native craft employed as such; but no vessels of considerable burden can come up to it from the want of sufficient depth of water.

The morning was foggy, so that we could not see the ship distinctly, and Sir Moses, who accompanied the captain in a boat long before the rest of the party, was directed to the ship by the compass. Before the anchor was raised and the ship cleared off, the fog had very much passed away, so as to afford a very good glimpse of the town, and some of the conspicuous buildings were pointed out to me by one of the young officers of the Magicienne, who had been some days at the port. The most remarkable of these was the old Portuguese Inquisition.

The Moorish Government twice sent a mona to the ship's crew, consisting of one bullock each time, a considerable number of fowls, alive, and an abundance of eggs and vegetables. The cattle on both occasions were so extremely out of condition, that, when killed, the flesh could not be made use of. I was told the carcase of the first was thrown away, and therefore suggested that the second should be taken alive to Tangier, and then put on shore and given away, and the proposal seemed to be assented to; but I learnt afterwards that the poor thing, a young bull, was killed and thrown away.

At Mazagan we parted with our escort and the greater number of our other travelling companions. They had been very civil and attentive, and were, no doubt, well pleased with the trip which they had made, and not less so with the generosity by which Sir Moses Montefiore, as usual, recompensed their services.

Almost to the last moment I had something to do in supplying medicines, lotions, or advice. There was no one who showed a greater inclination to stay with us than our very useful and intelligent Moorish carpenter.

The weather was beautifully fine, and as we approached and passed Cape Spartel, we had a good and not very distant view of the African coast, rising with rather an abrupt slope from the sea; and amongst the wooded summits of the hills, the country residences of Sir John Drummond Hay and T. Freeling Read were pointed out to us, whilst not far from them were the cultivated grounds of a resident of Tangier, beautifully situated to the south of the citadel. The Magicienne steered into the bay of Tangier, and remained for about two hours lying off the harbour, which gave an opportunity to several of the party to go on shore; but as we were informed that Sir John

Drummond Hay was absent, Sir Moses Montefiore concluded not to undergo the fatigue of landing, which, as there is no usable pier, he could not have effected without considerable trouble.

Our kind companion, T. Freeling Reade, hastened to his home; but finding that his wife and family had gone to Gibraltar, he felt himself at liberty to accompany us thither and join them.

Captain Armytage and some of the officers of the Magicienne, who had not before been in the port, were glad to avail themselves of the opportunity to take a transient view of the town.

Shalon Ferrache availed himself of the occasion to re-visit and take leave of his aged relatives and other friends. I was unwilling to lose the opportunity, and, like my companions, was again conveyed in a chair, carried by two persons, who had to wade for a considerable distance from the boat to the shore. The landing place was crowded by persons who had watched the arriving of the vessel, and I was presently greeted by several of my Tangier acquaintances, amongst whom I soon found Benzaqueen, whose kind attentions, and good knowledge of English, had been of great service to me on my former visit.

One of my chief objects on this occasion was to see the ruins of the Roman bridge, which I had previously in vain attempted to reach in one of my solitary walks. I found that with my friend's assistance, and by using a little activity, I might manage to go the distance—about two miles—and back again—before the Magicienne would leave the port; and I was well repaid for doing so, though the walk over the deep and loose sand was, in some places, really fatiguing.

On my return to the town, I had a short time to pay one or two visits before joining the ship.

We quitted the harbour, and the Magicienne seemed to put on extra speed, for we were so easily and quickly carried through the smooth water, that the excellent dinner to which we sat down, as we neared the Apes' Mountain, was scarcely finished when we found ourselves alongside the Quay at Gibraltar, from which we had previously sailed. Here we were met by several of our friends; Admiral Codrington was one of the first to greet Sir Moses.

At Gibraltar we were again lodged in the very convenient and well-situated house of A. E. Levy, which had been provided for Sir Moses' reception on his first visit. Here we spent several days very pleasantly. Sir Moses was closely occupied in receiving deputations, paying visits, and getting through a vast amount of correspondence, which various matters connected with his mission entailed upon him. At our dinner table we every day enjoyed the cheerful company of some of our friends, either from the Magicienne, before her leaving the port, or from Tangier, whence many of our Israelite acquaintances had come to pay their respects to Sir Moses; or from amongst the highly respectable Israelite merchants in Gibraltar. Our last meeting of this kind, on the eve of our departure for Malaga, was really a remarkable occasion, and I doubt not but it made a strong impression upon all those who were present. It was a sort of leave taking, to which many of the influential of the Israelite communities of Gibraltar and Tangier were invited.

Although the brilliant result of an arduous mission, undertaken under circumstances of sorrow and gloom, tended in no small degree to infuse a joyful feeling as we were seated at a sumptuous repast, there was, nevertheless, a prevailing seriousness at the approaching separation of so many sympathising friends. Sir Moses Montefiore, in addressing those about him, recalled to memory many interesting circumstances in connexion with his labours and travels for the relief or benefit of his brethren, and alluded to friends absent as well as present. Though it is improbable that anything like speech-making had been contemplated, some expression of feeling on the occasion was naturally called for. Our friend, Sampson Samuel, was particularly happy in his description of and comments on the scenes through which we had passed, and the persons who had taken part in them, in which his just tribute to the pervading kindness and other merits of our leader was particularly striking.

On such an occasion, poor speaker as I am, I could not remain silent, and as the only Christian present, I felt, as such, excited on the spur of the moment to give expression to some of the feelings which had impressed me during the course of the mission.

The words of my dear friend, Sir Moses Montefiore, recalled to mind the almost parental solicitude which, during the forty years of our acquaintance, I had experienced from himself and the late Lady Montefiore, kindness which I could not remember without emotion. Independent occasions of a professional character, during almost an equally long period, had brought me into more than ordinary intercourse with the Children of Israel, and I could not be insensible to the respect and kindness which they had invariably evinced towards me. I had, therefore, fully sympathised in the objects for which our expedition had been undertaken. I hoped I might be excused for offering a suggestion, to which my reflections had given rise, that successful as had been the perseverance of our leader in obtaining from the Sultan the edict which produced so much hope and joy, it would require continued vigilance, care, and caution that its object be not lost, but that the results which it was calculated to obtain might be fully realised. The Israelites of Morocco are a people who might render the greatest benefit to the country in which they live.

I alluded to the remarkable fulfilment of the prophecy that the Israelites should be as it were "sifted amongst the nations;" but I also remembered another prophecy to the effect that "they should be as a dew from heaven," and I believed that that also would be verified in such a manner as would prove acceptable both to Jews and Christians.

On the morrow, 25th, we embarked in good time in the morning on board the French steam packet for Malaga. Our Israelite friends were collected to take leave of us, and accompanied us to the quay, or even on board the vessel, and then themselves went on board another steamer which they had hired for the occasion, and, furnished with a band of music, accompanied us round Europa Point, and for some distance along the south side of the rock. The forenoon proved wet and gloomy; we were obliged to take shelter in the cabin, and our kind friends, whom we were sorry to see exposed to the wet, were constrained to bear round and part company long before they otherwise would have done. We soon lost sight of the African shore, and were prevented seeing as much of the coast of Spain as we otherwise should have done; yet, from time to time, when the weather permitted, we had some good glimpses of the shore and mountains behind it which give an undulating line to the horizon. As we neared Malaga in the afternoon, the Spanish hills looked truly grand and beautiful.

MALAGA.

THE object of Sir Moses in coming to Malaga was to avail himself of water communication with Alicant, whence there is a direct railway line to Madrid. When we arrived he was greatly disappointed to find that the information which he had received at Gibraltar was not correct (for the time being), and that none of the steamers from that port could further his progress towards Madrid without involving the necessity of either embarking or landing on the Sabbath.

We passed some days in Malaga before it was decided how we should proceed on our journey. At one time it was nearly arranged that we should return to Gibraltar and thence, by way of Algeziras to Cadiz, retrace our former route to Madrid.

It was an important object to avoid the fatigue inseparable from a long and rough road journey. On careful inquiry it was discovered that there was little if any appreciable difference in the amount of road travelling, whether we went by way of Granada or Cadiz. It was therefore concluded to engage a carriage, driver, and team to take us to Granada, with the option to continue their services to Santa Cruz de Mudela, or to send them back from Granada.

On the 27th, Sir Moses was sadly disappointed and fatigued, as we did not reach Loja, the first day's object, till after dark. The next day brought us to Granada easily, and in good time; but it had then to be fixed whether we should take the carriage or go on by diligence. Inquiries and perplexing deliberations occupied the greater part of the afternoon and evening, and at last it seemed to be decided not to take the diligence, but to keep to our carriage and proceed, after seeing the famed Alhambra. It was resolved to take a day of rest; for by no expedient haste could we reach Madrid for the Sabbath. Sir Moses was greatly fatigued, and S. Samuel not quite well, a return of an old and very painful malady made travelling, and even sight-seeing, distressing. The rest was, therefore, timely, and we hoped to be able to go forward on the morrow, intending to be sufficiently advanced on our route by the (sixth day) Friday afternoon, to take the railway from Santa Cruz de Mudela for Madrid on first day.

We visited the Alhambra, of which the specimen in the Crystal Palace gives a favourable and pretty accurate idea, except that it is on a reduced scale. This, and the interesting objects in its vicinity, and a visit to the Convent de los Martires, a rich monastery not now used, occupied a considerable time, and was about as much as we could well manage.

TOWARDS MADRID.

We were in motion before eight o'clock, and came to Campillo de Arenas in good time. We might have gone further had there been suitable accommodation on the route. The road had been good and the weather fine, but we were in a much lower temperature than we had been accustomed to.

The elevation was considerable, and snow-topped mountains were in our vicinity. Spanish inns, without fire-places, and with poor windows and doors, and brick floors, are not productive of creaturely comfort. Many circumstances attending our travelling were unfavourable to rapidity, though Sir Moses, Sampson Samuel, and myself were all desirous to make the best of our way home.

Sir Moses found land travelling on the common roads very fatiguing, and it did not answer for him to be in the carriage more than about six hours a-day, and exactly in that time suitable accommodation was not always to be found. On the sixth day (Friday), we necessarily stopped early, and on the seventh day, we rested completely. Crossing the Sierra Morena frequently reduced us to a walking pace, and we did not arrive at the railway station at Santa Cruz de Mudela till near the close of the first day (Sunday). Even then, Sir

Moses was inclined to go forward by the night train, which would have taken us to Madrid some time the following morning; but I persuaded him not to make the attempt, being in dread of the exposure as much as the fatigue for him. There is no inn at the station, but the station-master, who is known to Sir Moses' nephew, Weisweiller, recollected us, and was very kind and attentive, and made everything as comfortable as he could. The day train did not start till one o'clock, and we arrived at Madrid a little before eleven, when Sir Moses was much fatigued. The following day was almost incessantly wet, and I scarcely left the house, but was engaged in it. Sir Moses, however, made several calls, in the hope of expediting his business here. The following day the weather improved, though not without showers. I visited the museum, but could see but little, as on wet days some of the rooms are closed.

I also saw my brother's very worthy friend, Luis de Usoz i Rio, whom I found at home and well. Besides this I went to the water-works, which are under the management of a young friend from Cornwall. He was fortunately in the way. I pity his lonely situation, which is not one in which I should like to see any young person placed.

It was understood that the Queen would be churched on the 12th, and it was therefore probable that Sir Moses might, early in the week, be admitted to an audience. He much desired it, and was not likely to lose the chance. We were, therefore, still in uncertainty as to the day of our departure.

On the 10th the weather was fine, and being aware that we were not likely to be hurried away, S. Samuel and I took advantage of the opportunity to visit the ancient city of Toledo. J. Bache, the young friend at the water-works, kindly devoted the day to accompany us. We started about half-past six in the morning, the train leaving at seven a.m.

For a considerable part of the way our route by rail was the same as that by which we came from Santa Cruz de Mudela. We stopped for a short time at Aranjuez, where there is a summer palace of the Queen. The greater part of the way is flat, being apparently an alluvial water level; the soil, loam, or sand with much gypsum—some parts pretty well cultivated, others sadly neglected. We passed and crossed the Manzanares, which flows by Madrid, and after joining with another river, discharges itself into the Tagus, by the side of which we rode to Toledo, where we arrived about half-past ten o'clock, the station being about a mile from the town. The situation of this city is remarkably fine, which may account for its real antiquity, having been founded before, perhaps, even the Carthagenians invaded the country. Indeed the Spaniards themselves claim for this, their ancient capital, Tubal, the son or grandson of Japhet, as the founder. It stands on an elevated situation at the extremity of a range of hills, from which it is cut off by a chasm, through which the Tagus flows, having a hill with a fortress on its summit on the left, and the city, with its ruined palace, on the right The river passes under two bridges and then turns to the right, taking an almost retrograde direction across the plain lying on the other side of the city, which, being elevated, overlooks it to a great distance. Tall mountains, some of which are topped by snow, bound the horizon. In the same carriage by which we travelled was a Manchester clergyman, John G. Vance, who was spending the winter in the south on account of his health. He was our companion in our wanderings about the town. To enter we crossed an elevated bridge, and going by the ruins of a church, which must have been large and important, and under a gateway and tower at the extremity of the bridge, we ascended beside the ruined palace. A part of this ruin has been made habitable as a barrack, and a covered gallery connects its upper rooms with another building on the opposite side of the street, also devoted to soldiers — a College of Infantry.

Having breakfasted at an inn, we went to the cathedral, and engaged a guide already known to J. Bache. There are many side chapels, as in other Roman Catholic cathedrals, in which are rich tombs of remarkable persons connected with early Spanish history, such as prelates, governors, their wives, heads of royal houses, &c., &c. One of the most remarkable of these was a fighting bishop, who, having been victorious over Moors, has shells and a crescent on his coat of arms. I remember to have seen in the cathedral at Sienna a similar crescent on the escutcheon of Pope Æneas Sylvius, a Siennese. Some of the sculpture is remarkable for the fineness of the work rather than for the superiority of design, and is made of a very fine grained limestone, soft when fresh cut, but hardening by exposure. Near one of the doors is a colossal fresco of St. Christopher. A very remarkable piece of Roman Catholic superstition is an elevated lattice-work, or rather open-work covering, of a kind of pyramidal figure, enclosing the representation of the Virgin appearing in a fleshly form to invest the patron saint of the town and church. An inscription calls on the worshippers to adore on the spot which her feet had touched, and at the same time refers to a psalm in which the footsteps of the Almighty are mentioned. The stone pointed out is worn by the touches of the deluded. Whilst we were there a poor weak looking peasant listened to the story, touched the stone, and made a note in his pocket-book. In another place an inlaid piece of stone let into a column to designate the host having formerly been concealed within, is similarly defaced. The cathedral has one lofty tower or spire, which we ascended, and obtained a fine view of the surrounding country; it is used as a bell tower. There are several bells, and one of them of very remarkable

I

size; it appears to have been cracked, and, apparently to counteract the effects of this, an aperture has been cut, about an inch in breadth, through about half the height of the bell.

The clapper, not the bell, is swung, and there are several clappers at hand—one of bell metal, rather curiously cast, the others of wrought iron. We did not see the very rich jewels and relics, not being at the cathedral the right time of the day; but we went to the adjoining cloisters, which occupy the site of a market, in the olden time frequented by Jewish dealers. The sculptured stone and the frescoes with which they are ornamented are remarkable, though the latter are said to have been, with bad taste, substituted for others of far greater value which preceded them. Amongst the present is the representation of a child crucified, his side cut open, his heart removed and held in the hand of the executioner—an artistic effort of deceiving and deceived priests to incense their followers against the persecuted Jews.

Quitting the cathedral, our attention was called to a square tower, close to the church of San Tomé. It is obviously of Moorish work. Not only are the arches, near the top, of the Moorish form, but on some of the columns supporting them the green tiles are still remaining. We were taken to the local museum, an institution, such as all ancient cities ought to possess, in which relics of former periods are collected and preserved. Here, they chiefly consist of fragments of ecclesiastical sculpture, and of very numerous paintings, brought from suppressed monasteries. They are more remarkable as specimens of early art, of which they illustrate the progress, —and in some instances more from their subjects—than as masterpieces. Many, with all their stiffness, have the delicate and minute execution of miniatures, such as were executed before the time of Perugino. Others are portraits of remarkable persons, as of Cardinal Ximenes. And others show the strange conception of the monks by whom it is supposed they were painted. A painting of St. George and the Dragon is of this kind. The dragon, instead of being a huge beast, is, in proportion to the saint who is standing over him, about the size of a smallish dog, and its shape is a mixture of the human, the reptile, and the canine. Another curious point about it is, that the saint, who holds a sword in one hand, has a pair of scales, like a grocer's, in the other. It struck me that perhaps Milton might have seen a grotesque painting of this kind, and, from it, have taken the grand idea of the exhibition of Satan's impending fall in Libra, as he was about contending with the angel in Paradise, on being detected suggesting crime, in a dream, at the ear of Eve. In this museum there is a large piece of rather inferior Roman mosaic pavement, found under the roots of an olive tree in the neighbourhood of the city.

Continuing our walk quite across the town, we came upon an elevated terrace or promenade, just outside the walls, from which we had a view of this part of the city and its suburbs, and of the extensive plain lying on this side. Immediately below a rather abruptly-steep bank—but which, by taking a sloping direction, one may walk down—there is another promenade, which, in a part of its straight course, passes through the very imperfect remains of a work, supposed to be Roman, and to have been used as a circus. In one of the largest of the detached fragments is an opening, at a distance appearing like an arch, and there are also several other portions lying outside the limits of the ellipse. One of my companions suggested going below to inspect the ruins more closely, when we found the fragments to consist of rough masonry of unhewn stones, of no large size; yet it seemed pretty evident that there had been arches and arched passages, as in amphitheatres, for the support of covered seats, though there did not appear to have been many tiers. That which we took at a distance for an arch, seemed, when near, to have been an aperture broken through the external wall, and not of the original work, though traces of it seemed to exist elsewhere.

Our time being limited, and my companions waiting for me, I did not stop to make a sketch, but merely a hasty diagram, to give my conjecture as to the probable application of the neighbouring remains, which I imagine to have been a theatre, as the detached portions are so arranged as to form a large arc with a straight side. The promenade runs through the ellipse of the circus.

On this side of the city, but much more distant than the circus, is the celebrated manufactory for sword and dirk blades. They are hard and tough, and of such temper that they may be bent double, or rather, the point and hilt may be brought nearly or quite to touch without breaking. The point may be struck through a thick silver coin without breaking. We did not go to the manufactory, but a Swiss gentleman, who had just been there, shewed us the specimens which he had bought.

Going to the further extremity of the city, we looked down upon the Tagus below, having steep, rocky cliffs at its side, with occasional steep slopes down to it. Under the spot on which we stood, is an old tower, on the margin of the water. The guide connected it with a bath, and rumour with a doubtful and improbable story of Don Roderick, the last Gothic king. I imagine that a water-mill was formerly connected with the tower, as I observed a fragment of masonry rising out of the water at a suitable distance from the tower to give support to a water-wheel; and the position, in a rapid stream, seems much better suited to a mill than to a bath. We saw and crossed a second bridge, said to be Roman; but this is very doubtful. It has towers at each end, the construction of which is in part Moorish. We likewise visited two churches or chapels, which had been used as synagogues, and had been built by a wealthy Israelite family tolerated by the Moors. The first which we saw was confiscated by the Roman Catholic rulers, I think in 1405, the other some years later. Both are very good specimens of the Moorish style. The first has the least appearance of a synagogue, being divided into avenues by two rows of piers and Moorish arches. The piers are octagonal, with curiously-wrought capitals, on which are carved ornaments resembling pine cones. There are still a few Hebrew inscriptions, and the Mosaic fillagree is nearly entire, but whitewashed. The old arabesque wooden doors, with the Moorish hinges, are preserved in the church, and the interior of the roof, also of wood, appears to have escaped. It is probably but little used now, yet it has an altar and some other church furniture.

The second is very Moorish externally and internally, with the same style of building and ornament, well preserved, much resembling a modern synagogue—*e.g.*, at the upper part of the entrance end is the gallery for females. Opposite there is a kind of divan on each side, forming a part of the end itself, the seats and floor below still covered with variegated tiles. The walls are ornamented with filigree work, but with a modification, doubtless Jewish, which is ornamental and in good taste, since it produces a kind of frieze, in which the vine is conspicuous, and reminded me of the device on the Jerusalem coins of the Roman period. There were several inscriptions in the Hebrew character, some running nearly round the wall near the roof. The roof itself is of wood, like that in the other building. This chapel is in use. Here there are also Spanish coats of arms and old gilt church pictorial ornaments. One of them represents St. George and the

Dragon; something like that which I have already mentioned, but the dragon much larger in proportion, and with reptile form, combining something of the human female. The scales in the angel's hand have a little human figure in each cup. We were afterwards taken to see some well-preserved Moorish work, in a saloon or ball-room in the house of a private gentleman, who allows it to be inspected; also an old hall, in which is fine work, not so well preserved, seeing that it is used as a workshop, and violence and smoke have defaced it. Here, and in several other places, specimens of old woodwork and ironwork are worth noticing. Many of the old houses have porticos of granite, with columns of strong, but rude, workmanship. I should have said that the hill or rock on which the city stands, is of granite gneiss, and much of this stone, as well as limestone and brick, is used in the buildings. There is much appearance of ruin in almost every direction, partly from neglect and gradual dilapidation, partly—as in the case of the palace—from hostile violence, and in one or more large buildings from their not having been finished. We dined at Toledo, and took the evening train, after I had purchased a few photographs. Spanish trains are not conveniently arranged; there being only one morning and one evening train each way on the main line, so we had to wait in the midst of our return journey about half-an-hour or more, for the long and distant trains to come up. We, therefore, were as late as if we had come from Santa Cruz de Mudela.

We learned that the Queen was to make her public appearance on the 12th, at a church scarcely a mile out of the city, on the occasion of her recent confinement. She would have to pass our hotel in the Puerta del Sol. A public building, opposite to us, was illuminated in the evening, and cloth hung out from some of the windows. Many flags were displayed. In the morning, before eleven, troops began to pass and assemble—amongst them a long train of cavalry and artillery. Some of the royal carriages passed towards the Palace. Foot soldiers lined the route which the Queen was to take. Punctually at twelve, the Queen passed, preceded by several coaches, with six horses, and companies of horse guards. Some unmounted saddle horses were led in the procession, as when the Sultan received Sir Moses. On this day's occasion, one or more had side saddles. The Queen's carriage was immediately preceded by one drawn by eight horses, the same number that drew her own, which was distinguished by having a crown on the centre of the top. Her carriage, and one or two of the others, were gilt, and about as much glazed as our Lord Mayor's. I was too far off to have a good view of the Queen, yet I saw that the carriage contained a female with dark hair and dress, and a gentleman opposite, who was said to be the King. More than an hour after, the party returned, but in the meantime I had been out to make a call, and I saw the returning procession, or part of it, from the top of a house in which I was looking at photographs. The Queen had now made her public appearance, and there was great reason to presume that she would see Sir Moses either on the morrow or the next day.

We dined with Sir Moses' nephew and niece; the former is consul to the Bavarian and Wurtemburg Governments. Having just received the announcement of the death of the King of Bavaria, he had been obliged to put off a dinner which he had arranged to give to the foreign ministers, &c., in the evening. He and his wife have been very attentive to their uncle, and the former, who has a very good standing here, has been truly useful on behalf of the mission.

The Queen's late confinement, the ceremonies attendant on her getting about again, the death of the King of Bavaria, and the peculiar arrangements of the Spanish Court, which do not admit of the ministers seeing the sovereign, except on certain days, concurred to thwart Sir Moses in his wishes. Besides this, when actually travelling, the state of his health and strength limited our rate of progress; and the arrangements of the public conveyances, and the facilities for obtaining others were such as to throw impediments in our way.

Sir Moses had a second audience of the Queen of Spain, on Friday, March 18th, accompanied by his Excellency Sir J. F. Crampton. He presented to her Majesty a copy of the Imperial Edict of the Sultan of Morocco, with a translation in Spanish, which her Majesty most graciously received.

The following was the Memorial of SIR MOSES MONTEFIORE, Bart., addressed to the SULTAN OF MOROCCO, and His Majesty's Reply:—

COPY OF MEMORIAL

Presented to His Sheriffian Majesty, the Sultan of Morocco, on Monday, the 24th day of Sebat, 5624 (1st February, 1864), by SIR MOSES MONTEFIORE, BART., who was accompanied by MOSES NAHON, ESQ., of Tangier, THOMAS FELLOWES READE, ESQ., Consul to Her Britannic Majesty at Tangier, CAPTAIN WILLIAM ARMYTAGE, of H.M.S. the " Magicienne," SAMPSON SAMUEL, ESQ., and DR. THOMAS HODGKIN, etc., etc.

TO HIS SHERIFFIAN MAJESTY THE SULTAN OF MOROCCO.

May it please your Majesty,—

I come supported by the sanction and approval of the Government of her Majesty the Queen of Great Britain, and on behalf of my co-religionists in England, my native country, as well as on the part of those in every part of the world, to entreat your Majesty to continue the manifestation of your Majesty's grace and favour to my brethren in your Majesty's empire.

That it may please your Majesty to give the most positive orders that the Jews and Christians dwelling in all parts of your Majesty's dominions shall be perfectly protected, and that no person shall molest them in any manner whatsoever in anything which concerns their safety and tranquillity: and that they may be placed in the enjoyment of the same advantages as all other subjects of your Majesty, as well as those enjoyed by the Christians living at the ports of your Majesty's empire. Such rights were granted through me by his Imperial Majesty Abdul Medjid, the late Sultan of Turkey, by his firman given to me at Constantinople, and dated 12th Ramazan, 1256; and in the month of May last confirmed by his Imperial Majesty Abdul Aziz, the present Sultan of Turkey.

Permit me to express to your Majesty my grateful appreciation of the hospitable welcome with which your Majesty has honoured me, and to offer to your Majesty my heartfelt wishes for your Majesty's health and happiness, and for the prosperity of your Majesty's dominions.

COPY OF THE IMPERIAL EDICT.

Under the Seal and Signature of His Sheriffian Majesty, the Sultan of Morocco, delivered to SIR MOSES MONTEFIORE, BART., at the City of Morocco, on Friday, the 28th day of Sebat, 5624 (5th February, 1864).

IN THE NAME OF GOD, THE MERCIFUL AND GRACIOUS.

There is no power but in God, the high and mighty. (L.S.)

BE it known by this our Royal Edict—May God exalt and bless its purport and elevate the same to the highest heavens, as he does the sun and moon!—That it is our command that all Jews residing within our dominions, be the condition in which the Almighty God has placed them whatever it may, shall be treated by our Governors, Administrators, and all other subjects, in manner conformable with the evenly balanced scales of justice, and that in the administration of the Courts of Law, they (the Jews) shall occupy a position of perfect equality with all other people, so that not even a fractional portion of the smallest imaginable particle of injustice shall reach any one of them, nor shall they be subjected to anything of an objectionable nature. Neither they (the authorities) nor any one else shall do them (the Jews) wrong, whether to their persons or to their property. Nor shall any tradesman among them, or artisan, be compelled to work against his will. The work of every one shall be duly recompensed, for injustice here is injustice in heaven, and we cannot countenance it in any matter affecting either their (the Jews') rights or the rights of others, our own dignity being itself opposed to such course. All persons in our regard have an equal claim to justice, and if any person should wrong or injure one of them (the Jews), we will, with the help of God, punish him.

The commands hereinbefore set forth have been given and made known before now, but we repeat them, and add force to them, in order that they may be more clearly understood, and more strictly carried into effect, as well as serve for a warning to such as may be evilly disposed towards them (the Jews), and that the Jews shall thus enjoy for the future more security than hithertofore, whilst the fear to injure them shall be greatly increased.

This decree, blessed by God, is promulgated on this 26th of Shaban of the year 1280. (5th February, 1864.)—Peace!

On the morning of the 21st of March (third month), we safely entered France, which, after Spain, appeared something like home, and was at least a country whence home is much more accessible. We had no more travelling difficulties in anticipation, but good railways all the route, except for crossing the Channel. We started from Madrid about nine a.m., on the 20th; and much as I had dreaded the journey for Sir Moses he performed the task, which he had imposed on himself, without stopping to rest. Before we reached Avila, an accident to the rails, caused by heavy rains, stopped our course, and delayed us about two hours. We had some distance to walk to a set of carriages beyond the injured part, and all the luggage had to be carried. We had also twice to change, from train to diligence, which latter did not always travel the best of roads. Sir Moses was, of course, very much fatigued.

We left Bayonne on the 22nd, passing through Bordeaux, and arrived at Paris late on the 24th.

Sir Moses having determined to make the whole journey from Bordeaux to Paris in one day, as the only means by which he could advance his objects, it gave him the greater part of the next day, thus enabling him to see our ambassador, through whom he hoped to obtain an early interview with the Emperor.

On the first of fourth month, 1864, Sir Moses was, by appointment, at the Tuileries a little after one o'clock. He was shewn into the waiting-room looking upon the large square of the Louvre (Place Carousel), I accompanied him. A very pleasing gentleman soon came in, and said that the appointed time had not quite arrived, but that the Emperor would shortly be ready. About half-past one, a waiter, in livery, entered, inviting us to go to the Emperor. Sir Moses stated that my name had not been mentioned, and asked whether I should accompany him, upon which the messenger signified that both should follow him. We were shewn into a waiting-room, a more completely furnished apartment, looking on to the garden. There we found the gentleman who had before spoken to Sir Moses, who explained that the Emperor had been a little delayed at his breakfast. To this gentleman Sir Moses again addressed the question, whether I should join in the audience, explaining that I had been his companion on the journey to Morocco, and again he was assured the Emperor would be pleased to receive me.

His Majesty the Emperor received most graciously a copy of the firman granted by the Sultan of Morocco in compliance with the petition which Sir Moses had presented to him.

This interesting and important document assures the equal protection of the law to the Israelites of Morocco, in common with the other subjects of the Sultan, and is couched in terms strongly evincing the excellent intentions of his Sheriffian Majesty.

After this successful termination to the mission we left Paris, and soon arrived safely at home.

ADDENDA.

ADDENDA.

I HOPE the interest which a transient visit to the Empire of Morocco has raised in my own mind may not have misled me in inducing a belief that a few extracts, which I have been kindly permitted to make from notes of travellers, who have also visited the country, and have seen parts to which I did not go, may be acceptable to my readers. It is greatly to be desired that England should have more intimate and more extensive intercourse with Morocco, and that its present relations should be somewhat modified, although even now, thanks to Sir John Drummond Hay, our present minister there, and to our late Consul-General, Thomas F. Reade, our relations with the Government are of the most friendly and cordial kind, a fact Sir Moses Montefiore, and we who accompanied him, can fully testify, as well as to the courtesy and liberality with which we were received by the Sultan, his ministers, and the people generally. Nevertheless, a certain degree of shyness towards strangers is evidently existing amongst them.

The productions of the country manifestly admit of a very great increase, both in quantity and quality; and, could the Government be induced to promote these improvements, and at the same time to facilitate transport within the empire, and commercial transport from it, the Sultan's revenue, and the comfort and happiness of his subjects of all classes, might be almost incalculably increased.

Besides making the following extracts, I have endeavoured to obtain some further information regarding the remarkable covering of a tufa, or travertin, formation (hitherto, I believe, altogether unnoticed) which I traced from Mogador to the city of Morocco, but which must extend far beyond it, and from that city to Mazagan.

Archibald Fairley has told me that he traced it to Rabat, considerably further to the north, and that he again found it when travelling between Mequinez, about forty miles to the north of that city.

The son of our late Vice-Consul at Mogador, C. Elton, has informed me that the travertin, in a stalactitic form, is to be found a little to the north of Mogador, and that the specimens there are much finer than those which attracted my attention near Debat, a little further south, and which were the only specimens of the kind I observed.

Extracted by permission from Notes on Morocco, made by Archibald Fairley, civil engineer, employed by the Sultan:—

Alcazar is about three days' journey from Tangier, or, say, seventy miles, and is apparently one of the oldest cities in Northern Africa, or, more properly speaking, in the Morocco Empire. It is situated at the head of a level plain, close to some hills which nearly surround it, and which are on the north-east and south of it. The town is exceedingly flat, and consequently the drainage very imperfect, which, in warm weather, causes very bad smells to arise.

The city is built of bricks of the same pattern as the old Roman; they are well burnt in kilns. The ordinary soil, mixed with water, acts the part of mortar for cement. The houses are very narrow, and roofed as in Europe. In no other city that I have seen in Morocco is this the case. The streets are, on an average, about from six to eight feet wide, and are very dirty. The houses are, for the most part, two stories high; some have inner courts, but this is not universal. There are ten very ancient, and ten modern mosques, with lofty square towers. The vegetation surrounding this city is exceedingly rank, from the fertilising effects of the drainage, but the coarse nature of the grass, resembling reeds, makes it useless for pasture. In the rainy season it is almost impossible to approach the town, from there being no paved roads.

The river Wad-lo-Koos, which passes within half a-mile of

the town, was, in June, when I crossed it, about two hundred and fifty feet wide, with a running stream of about one and a half to two knots an hour; the depth of water was, in the centre, about three feet, and the banks were about thirty feet above the level of the river. I saw no bridge crossing it; all traffic has to ford it.

The population of Alcazar is estimated at about twenty-six thousand, including about two thousand Jews. The general character of the population is similar to that of Morocco.

There are a few fundicks, or caravanserais, where the trade and commerce of the town are carried on.

About forty miles from Tangier, on the road to Mequinez, there are ancient stone works,* having very much the Druidical character, inasmuch as the stones are all placed on end, and forming a circle of about seventy yards in diameter. The two large, high stones, which form, as it were, two gate-posts, and look due west, were respectively eighteen and sixteen feet high, of an oval shape, being at the base four feet by two feet six inches. The total number of stones still maintaining a vertical position is eighty; they are of a red sandstone. The interior is in the shape of a mound, raised some twenty feet high in the centre, with a flat top of about thirty feet in diameter. I could not get any information from my soldiers or the Arabs living about as to the origin of it, nobody knowing any more of it, than that it has been there time out of mind.

* There are several other ruins having something of a Druidical character in the northern part of Morocco. In Sir J. Drummond Hay's portfolio, which he showed me when I was in Tangier, is a drawing of some large stones of this kind; but they were few in number, and not to be compared with the circles seen and described by Archibald Fairley.—T. H.

From Alcazar to Mequinez is four days' journey, or one hundred miles; the country for the first two days is exceedingly flat, very fertile, but destitute of trees. Within two days of Mequinez the road, or track, winds in amongst some very fine hills, which continue up to the city. About twelve miles from it is the city of Muley Dris, celebrated as being the last resting-place of the great saint of that name, and also because neither Christians nor Jews have ever been allowed to set foot within its walls. It is very romantically situated on the side of a mountain, and is surrounded with olive groves, and is supplied with an abundance of splendid water. The population is estimated at thirty thousand.

In going from Alcazar to Mequinez, I crossed the magnificent river called the Seboo, which is eminently suited for navigable purposes—its width, from bank to bank where I passed over would be about two hundred yards, the banks rising almost perpendicularly from the water, and between thirty and forty feet high, the soil being a rich alluvial. The river swarms with fish, but no attempts are made to catch them. I saw thousands swimming listlessly on the top of the water, between two and three feet long, of the white salmon species. The depth of water was, when I crossed it, in June, about eight feet, which might be taken as a mean for the year. I went over this river in a large ferry boat, no bridge* being

* Although neither Archibald Fairley nor Captain Hood saw any bridge across the river Seboo, I have been informed by an Israelite, who had long resided and travelled in that part of Morocco, that there are nearly or quite a dozen bridges by which that river is crossed. This is by no means improbable, as there are well-built bridges near Morocco, and one in particular, of several arches, across the Tensift.—T. H.

nearer than Fez. In the rainy season all traffic is suspended, in consequence of the great danger and risk incurred in fording this stream. Several lives are annually lost in trying to cross when journeying from Fez or Mequinez to Tangier. Could this river only be made to send a little of its water over the surrounding country, it would make it a land literally flowing with milk and honey, in fact, a Paradise.

Fez is about one day, or thirty miles, to the east of Mequinez, and is a large, straggling city, with numerous mosques of the most magnificent description—one of them being a fac-simile of the Cordova Cathedral. The streets are wider than those of any city I have seen in Barbary, and are certainly the cleanest, although entirely unpaved. All the houses are whitewashed, and are of a superior build to those of Morocco. The people are much whiter than those of the capital, and appear to have a better idea of business matters than any I have met with in this country. There are several large manufactories in it for the production of silks, slippers, haicks, burnooses, sword blades, pottery, &c., and the red caps, called after the city. This place supplies Egypt and a portion of Turkey with the products mentioned. The gardens of Fez are very fine and very large, and immense quantities of fruit are grown in them. Both Fez and Mequinez are built on high table-land, and in most commanding positions—the climate of both being unsurpassed for its salubrity. The population is estimated at about one hundred and eighty thousand souls. The fruit consists of oranges, the finest in the world, grapes, melons, apples, pears, plums, sweet and sour lemons, pomegranates, mulberries, walnuts, olives, and dates.

Extracted, by permission, from the Journal kept by Captain A. N. Hood, when in company of Sir J. D. Hay, on an Embassy to the Sultan of Morocco, at Mequinez, 1861.*

Our party started from Tangier, Wednesday, 11th of July; after twelve o'clock stopped at a fountain on a hill, called Dar-el-Klow. From this hill we saw several miles ahead; then forded a deep salt river; the road bad, through a steep, hilly country. Met the English Consular Agent from Laraish, and halted for the night at the village Had-el-Garbia. We had had six and a-half hours' travelling. The people played on instruments, resembling clarionets, with hautboy reeds.

12th.—Turned out at 4 a.m., started at 5·30. Kept to the top of a range of low hills, well cultivated; at 7·30 left the hills for a large plain. Halted at ten, and started again at twelve; rode through a hilly country covered with brushwood. Stopped for the night at Gók-el-Hatsaraisana.

13th.—Started at 5·30; passed through a large wood of small cork trees. Forded deep water, and rested from eight till nearly twelve. The river we passed is called Wad-el-Warood. It enters the Atlantic at Laraish, and is called El Koos (the bow). It is the Luccus of the Romans. Came in sight of Alcazar, a large town, outside the walls of which a crowd of about two thousand persons were awaiting our arrival. We passed through the town; streets narrow;

---

* The native tribes, at the end of the mission, were averse to paying their taxes, without which the Sultan would be unable to find the money which by the late treaty he was bound to pay to Spain.
Captain Hood went as photographer.—T. H.

houses red brick, not whitewashed. Crossed a river with very high banks, and camped outside the town on a ploughed field.

14th (Sunday).—Started at 5·15. The country pretty; brushwood on the hills; cultivation plentiful—many cattle. Mountains of a beautiful blue colour to the east. Road rather stony; but a dog-cart might have done the whole journey. Met by a large Kabyla tribe at 7·30, and at nine, by a great man, Basha Benoda, with four hundred cavalry and six hundred infantry. At 9·30, Basha Hahassa met us with four hundred attendants. Came to a beautiful bubbling spring (water 70 deg.). Finished the day's journey, sixteen miles, at ten o'clock.*

15th.—Ther. at sunrise, 59 deg. Started at 5·20. Dead level plain, for six miles across, up to the river Seboo, the largest in this part of Barbary, and navigable for boats to Fez. Steamers might ply the whole distance; the water a deep yellow; the bottom soft mud; encamped on its banks —the wind high and threatened damage to the tents.

16th.—Tents and baggage taken over the river in boats and the horses swam—they and the mules, ninety-one in number. The Boni Hassan, a wild tribe, escorted us. Started at 7·30, the ground flat and evidently wet in winter. The chief, Ben Amra, one of the handsomest men in the country. One tribe adopt the Berber custom of wearing large tufts of hair over their temples, which, sticking out

---

* The journal contains particulars of visits, the provisions supplied by chiefs on the Sultan's account, and a description of tax collecting, &c.—T. H.

under the turban, give somewhat of a European appearance, which the Moors, who shave their heads entirely, have not, or the Reefians, who leave a thin scalp-lock. These tribes are very warlike, and continually keep down their superfluous energy, by fighting with their neighbours, the Azimur. The horses were splendid. We passed the Seboo several times. It is a very winding stream. There was not much cultivation the first part of the journey, but we saw great numbers of cattle feeding. Later in the day we passed through barley-fields which extended right and left as far as we could see. This plain was a most interminable affair. We saw a white building, the tomb of a saint, Leed Bokhary, and were told that it was to be our camp. As we approached, it seemed to recede. There were twelve hundred of the Scherrurde tribe waiting to receive us. This is a militia, or half-regular tribe of cavalry.

17th.—En route at 5·30. Ten miles of flat on account of a river—not a breath of air—dust very thick—the sun overpowering—Barley and wheat not very extensively cultivated—several wells—the neighbourhood stony and barren—pitched our camp on the banks of Wad-el-Koumal. We rode in at twelve o'clock. Thermometer one hundred deg. in the mess-tent—occasionally a whirlwind passing through—prepared for entering Mequinez the next morning.

18th.—Up at three a.m., started at four—crossed the river Koumal, and went up a steep hill—day broke at 4·40—found ourselves on a plain on high ground, with mountains on our left, about four miles distant—passed the town of Tartron, four miles west of the mountains—the population ragged and rude. We came suddenly to the end of the plain and found ourselves on the top of a high and very steep hill; a beautiful plain below us cultivated with grain and olive trees. Saw Mequinez nine miles distant on an elevated plateau. The minarets looked very fine, rising from amidst the masses of white houses and red walls. We observed an Arab on a magnificent white horse; made a persevering effort to obtain the animal, and succeeded in making a bargain for thirty pounds sterling, with a warranty to be brought with the horse, the promise was never performed. After fording a small deep stream, we turned suddenly to the right, and went up hill on to what seemed a continuation of the high ground on which the town is built. Here an increasing crowd joined our party, and kept with us, much to our inconvenience, from dust, noise, &c.; horses fine, men handsome, well armed, although their clothes were rather ragged.

The way becoming narrower we were suddenly pushed through a small gate, and found ourselves in a road about thirty yards wide, well watered. The walls on each side of us were about twenty-four feet high, and covered with spectators, all men, of course. We passed through several gates, and at each our escort stopped some of the crowd that followed us; at last, after passing through a bazaar, which was shut up, the last gate was closed against every one except our own soldiers, and some of the principal officers who were riding with us. We rode through narrow streets, not very well kept. The tops of the houses were covered with women, carefully rolled up in blankets, who were looking out for us. Then we entered the large court outside the castle or palace, where the soldiers play powder. The gate of the palace, at the end of the square, is magnificent. It is a building of about forty feet high, and fifty yards long, covered with inlaid tiles in patterns, and marble columns along the front. The gateway itself is very wide. We rode on through a few narrow streets and two bazaars, and at last arrived at our appointed residence. We passed through the little hall or guard-room, and entered the court-yard. It is about forty-five feet square, the floor inlaid with coloured tiles, with a fountain of rather muddy water in the middle. The verandah of the upper story is supported by tall pillars, and arches covered with filigree-work in plaster. We went up stairs, attended by an old Moor, Abderahman Aga, who had, the previous year, been to London with the Moorish Embassy. We found a table laden with sweetmeats, and bread and butter; some slaves brought tea and coffee, and then we were left to ourselves to explore the house.

There were three rooms up stairs, with large folding doors opening into the verandah. The floors were all tiled. The rooms were hung with silk and damask; large iron bedsteads, made in the European fashion. One large dining table was laid out in the passage, in which were several chairs. The three rooms down stairs were apportioned to our soldiers and servants. There was a large bath-room and fountain.

The top of the house was, of course, flat, and we rushed up in hopes of getting a view of the town, and of the Moorish beauties; but we found a wall all round the place from seven to ten feet high, with only a few loop-holes, so narrow that one could scarcely see anything. However, the whole female population had turned out on the roofs. With our glasses we were enabled to discover some nice looking women. All those that seemed to belong to the higher classes were horribly painted, rouged, streaks of black paint between their eyes down the nose, patches on their cheeks, and, in some cases lines on their foreheads; hands stained, with purple or white lines on the backs of them. Moorish etiquette required that we should rest three days before seeing the Sultan, and that we should not walk out of our house.

19th.—Engaged in writing letters, copying despatches, &c., &c.

20th.—Ditto. The confinement irksome.

21st (Sunday).—Service at 10·30; repetition of the two preceding days.

22nd.—Paraded in full dress for an interview with the Sultan. Our party rode; but all the Moors were on foot. The streets had all been watered; we passed between two lines of soldiers through two large court-yards until we arrived at the Meshwa, or large court of the palace, which we found full of soldiers. There were more than two hundred of the Moorish troops ranged round the court-yard two deep; and on two sides of the square, at the back, there were nine hundred men, armed in European fashion, green knickerbockers, bare legs, slippers, blue and red coats, and Fez caps, muskets, bayonets, and swords. Then a large gate opposite opened to us, and the procession began. First came the Kaid al Meshwa and his staff, two by two; then a number of Kaids, or officers of the palace; then six led horses, two white, two grey, a black, and a bay—fine animals, but rather sinewy; next followed two men with long lances, a weapon not now used among the Moors, but with which their ancestors conquered the country; after these the Sultan, mounted on a large white horse with high action, but such big legs! green bridle and reins, green silk saddle, and gilt stirrups and bit. His Imperial Majesty was dressed in white, the hood of his burnoose pulled well over his head. The only appearance of royalty in his costume were large silk tassels on his hood.

Behind the Sultan came the state executioner, carrying a broad sword, then the Sheriffian umbrella, held by an Officer of State. The Sultan is the only follower of the prophet who is allowed to shelter himself from the rays of the sun with an umbrella. More officers and soldiers closed the procession.

The Sultan rode straight up to us. Mr. Hay made a speech in Spanish, which was translated by the interpreter of the mission, David Siesa, a Tangier Jew. The Sultan said we were welcome. Mr. Hay then presented the Queen's letter; the Sultan took it. We were all presented. His Majesty said complimentary things, and went off. (This ceremony took place before breakfast.)

An evening party was given at the Prime Minister's at ten p.m. The walls of his house are ornamented like those of the Alhambra. The floors inlaid tiles—a fountain in the middle —many wax candles, and incense burning—music.*

At twelve p.m. the party were carried off to another much larger house, brilliantly illuminated with more than three hundred lamps. Two large balconies overlooked the courtyard, and were filled with, at the least, a hundred veiled women.

23rd.—The Emperor had a private interview of more than an hour with Mr. Hay, after which we visited the garden and park, in which were mares and foals, gazelles, sheep, and ostriches; I found an ostrich's egg. On a late occasion the Sultan sent us four, new laid, which formed a gigantic omelette in taste like that of other eggs. About a week was passed in rather a monotonous way—the thermometer seldom below 80 deg., except just before sunrise.

We had some good shooting in the evenings.

August 4th.—A storm of dust and little stones, followed by rain, for three quarters of an hour. The Sultan sent word that we could not go to Fez, the Governor being dead and the people unruly. This was much to be regretted, as Fez was only about thirty miles off, and is the finest town in that part of Morocco.

5th.—A very hot day. Ther. 86 deg. at breakfast; at twelve, 107 deg. in the shade on the roof. Had a very

* Captain Hood remarked that some notes seemed to be wanting in their scale; and that he was unable to make out clearly a whole octave.—T. H.

agreeable ride in the evening to a holy well, from which we drank most delicious water. We returned along the banks of the main sewer of the town.

6th.—Some snake charmers were brought to us to-day. Three dirty men, with a basket of snakes, and two large tambourines, nearly as large, and quite as noisy, as a big drum. The men played vigorously on their tambourines, and the snakes danced about. One man made a snake bite his nose, until it bled profusely. Another took up a large reptile and, after saying a prayer to Assa, the saint of snake-charmers, told the snake to kiss his eyes and his face, which it did, very gently. After which he called the snake some name, and it struck at him and hung on his nose. On pulling it off, he also bled. Mr. Hay said he knew the snakes were of a venomous kind. I bought some "keef," which has the same effect on the Moors as opium has on the Chinese. It had no effect on me.

7th.—Ther. 94 deg. at breakfast. The Sultan sent a religious sect, called the "Hamacha," to amuse us. They were wild and dirty-looking people. The chief man was a Negro, dressed in an old leather tunic and a leopard skin, his cap embroidered with cowries and ostrich feathers. They carried big clay drums on their shoulders, which made an intolerable noise. They began singing and drumming quietly enough; but the black man very soon became excited and rushed round the court-yard, yelling like a maniac. All the time we were safe up in our gallery, looking down upon the dancers. David, the interpreter, and his Jewish servant took refuge with us, and our soldiers did sentry at the foot of the stairs and at the top. The dancers became more and more frantic. The black rushed about, howling and shouting for a sword, which was given to him. He danced harder than ever, and hit himself on the head with the edge of the sword, until he was covered with blood. There was no deception. His forehead and the top of his head were terribly mangled. He then got a hatchet, sat down, and, laying the sword on the calf of his leg, hammered it with the hatchet. But his leg was so hard and the sword so blunt, that he did not do much execution with it. About this time he was perfectly rabid. One of our servants, who was looking on, began to assist in playing the drums. Then he helped to sing their hymns, and at last he got more excited than anybody—threw off his clothes, and danced more wildly than any, excepting the black. His principal fancy was to get earthern pots, throw them high in the air, and let them fall on his head and smash or not, according to their thickness. When a large earthen jar was too heavy to lift, he went at it like a ram, and sent his head through it. He cut himself badly at this game. A respectable old Kaid, in command of the guard, who had been restraining the dancer's impetuosity as much as possible, and who had saved a great deal of our crockery from utter destruction, suddenly took mad himself. The old man must have been between seventy and eighty, and yet he was, for a short time, more active than any of them. At last he fell down exhausted, and the others danced a war-dance round him, while the black cut his head open again and made savage but ineffectual attempts on his legs. Again they set to, and finished by wallowing in the fountain. Then they all stopped and sang hymns, and dried their drums over a charcoal fire; after which they danced, and prayed, and drummed, but much quieter than before, until the old man, who had dressed himself and got quiet, recommenced worse than ever, but after a while subsided in the fountain. The black was so far subdued that he was lying down in a corner, yelling and howling like mad. After an hour of this fun Mr. Hay sent them some money, as a hint to go. They all prayed and burnt incense for our future welfare, and then sang a soothing hymn; and if any one tried to break out again and dance, he got hit over the head and stopped. Then they prayed for old Jelaly, and after getting the whole party pretty sensible (except the black, who bolted yelling) they went off after making their best bows.

The black was tremendously cut about. Besides the sword and hatchet he had got a lamp wick, steeped in oil, which, having lighted, he proceeded to roast himself. He held this flaming wick for five minutes under his chin and at the back of his knees. No Christians ever saw the whole ceremony before, and it was a great mark of the Sultan's favour sending these men to us. The business was religious, but not connected with Islamism. They were all Mohammedans; but their Saint is an outsider. The way they revive one of their body in a trance is by whispering in his ear "There is but one God," then the man gets up and is rational.

10th.—The German Doctor Kohlss came to see us with his interpreter, who spoke French. I talked to him about the disciplined troops here; he said there were from four to five thousand infantry, and five hundred artillery men, with about fifty pieces of field artillery, of which a few were English and good; the rest were honey-combed, and frequently burst.

13th.—Everything being now arranged, we paraded in uniform, for the last time, to take leave of the Sultan. We rode to the palace, dismounted, and walked into the garden, and were received by the Sultan in a small summer-house, with no furniture but a horse-hair sofa, half worn out, on which his Majesty was squatted cross-legged. He was very complimentary, and said he regretted that, owing to the unsettled state of his country, he could not show us as much sport as he wished, yet, if we came after he had settled his little bills with the refractory tribes, he would be glad to see us and give us more amusement. We bowed and retired.

14th.—Left Mequinez at 5·30 a.m. to encamp at Schenarde. After some travelling the party bore away more to the right, or N.E., to visit the ruins of Casbar Pharaoh, the King's Castle, or Pharaoh's Castle. We went on the high level plain at the foot of the Zarhon hills. These hills were beautiful in the morning sun. The mists had not quite cleared off, and the woods up the hills, and Zarhon up one of the ravines, appeared most picturesque. At 9·30 we arived at the ruins.

L

Very little remains standing of what seems to have been a very large building; three arches alone are left. The ground for half-a-mile round is covered with large hewn stones. No mortar seems to have been used in the building. Our tent was pitched by the side of the river Khoumal, close to the ruins.

We started again at one o'clock. The heat of the sun was intense—it makes me hot to think of it; and the wind was even hotter than the sun; thermometer 107 deg. in the shade of our tent. The water, by the way, was deficient and not good, but a supply might be obtained by digging. Reached, at last, the Boni Hassan plain, not far from where we encamped on the 16th July. We got to camp at seven, having had thirteen and a half hours' journey.

15th.—Up at four, in the saddle at five. We crossed the Seboo on horseback. It was not deep; but the stream was strong.

16th.—Started at 4·50 for a long day's march. We were taken to where we had encamped on the 14th July; arrived there at 7·30, and found a large tent, and a bountiful supply for breakfast; started again at nine for Alcazar. We were met by a dirty, half naked man outside the town, by whom we were conducted round to a garden, in which we found wretched accommodation and poor supplies, with which we and our Moorish companions were not well pleased.

Started from Alcazar at 4·30, and having been misled on our way, arrived at six o'clock at our evening encampment on the banks of the Wad-el-M.-Hassan; bathed among tortoises and frogs. The neighbouring tribe, the Kloté, did not send their contributions of food until ten p.m.; the evening cool.

17th.—Started at 5·30; passed a large wood at Sok-el-Hatsa at 12·30; after quick riding halted in an olive wood until 4·30; at six o'clock arrived at Had-el-Garbia, near an old Portuguese fountain.

18th (Sunday).—Up at 2·30 for an early start at 3·10; crossed the river without accident, and reached the foot of Dar-el-Klow by day-break; crossed the hill without adventure, and had a view of the Tangier hills from the top. Near Arbacherun we were met by our Tangier friends, and when we reached the city our party separated in the market place, surrounded by a great crowd, having taken leave of each other in due form.

Extract of a letter from A. Fairley, dated Rabat, 18th October:—

"On the morning of the 13th September, when I arrived at the 'Fabrica,' the name of the sugar mill and buildings at Morocco, I found that considerable preparations had been made and were making, for a great feast. The floor was covered with very rich carpets, with a few round leather cushions (fac-similes of which you have seen at Tangiers); there were also several trays, similar to those of Hadji Said, silvered or electro-plated, on which were placed the tea things. At a distance from the carpets were four charcoal fires, similar in shape to the 'devils' used in engine sheds. On these fires were kettles, getting the water ready, &c. I had just finished my inspection when the Basha arrived, with about thirty or forty of his friends, who came to help to eat the good things which he had had prepared for the purpose. Added to these guests, there were also about one hundred and fifty soldiers, who had to share in demolishing the food.

"Operations were commenced with tea, and then tea and meat, and bread and honey, and tea again. Whilst this was going on, a whole string of the Basha's soldiers came, each man carrying on his head a round wooden tray, about the size of a sieve, and the same depth of side or rim. In, or rather on, these trays were placed the solids, in dishes about the size of wash-hand basons, the whole surmounted by a cover, in shape exactly like the hat worn by Mother Redcap, in Camden Town, and made of rushes. These soldiers came opposite the Basha (there were twenty of them); they each placed his dish on the ground, and on a signal being given, all the lids, or covers, were simultaneously taken off, and disclosed the contents for the inspection of their master, who glanced his eye right along, and then nodded assent. The covers were immediately replaced, and the things carried on one side, there to await the attack. Some of these dishes contained meats of various kinds, all apparently stewed; others contained bread, and others the great dish of Morocco, 'Koos-ko-soo;' in fact it as much the national dish as the 'olla podrida' of Spain, the 'roast beef' of England, the 'spuds 'of Ireland, or the 'haggis' or 'porridge' of Scotland.

"You must bear in mind that we were not all drinking out of one pot. There were several little circles of nine or ten persons, who had tea apparatus for themselves, but who did no movement without seeing that the Basha showed the initiative. We will put away the tea things, and bring in the 'kabobs' (I think that is the name). These things are particularly nice, and were some enterprising cook-shop keeper to introduce them into London, I think a fortune would be the result. They are made of very finely chopped or minced meat, with parsley, &c., which is wrapped round a stick for about eight inches, the stick being about eighteen inches by half-inch in diameter, and the meat wrapped round to the thickness of about one to one-eighth of an inch in diameter; it is then held over a charcoal fire, and continually turned for some minutes and served in one of the basins aforesaid and placed before the Basha. He took up a stick with his fingers, broke off a bit of the end, tasted it, and then—oh horror! put the remaining piece into my mouth. Being the guest of the day, of course I had no remedy but to swallow it, and put on as smooth a face as I possibly could, although I must confess it was considerably against the grain.

"After this little preliminary and interesting performance the Basha handed a fresh stick to me from the wash-hand basin (which I would rather he had done in the first instance), as well as one all round, and took another himself. As I before mentioned, these 'Kabobs' are really delicious. A piece of bread is held in the left hand, the stick in the right, biting alternately until all the meat be eaten off. By this time another dish is served, another stick is taken, and so on, until one cries 'Hold, enough!' After clearing away, a slave comes round with soap and water to wash hands, another following with a towel; then preparations are made to bring in the 'Koos-koo-soo,' which is served in the basins, one of which being placed before the Basha, he plunged his hand in, took out some, and by remarkably dextrous tosses he transformed the mass into a ball, and then transferred it to his mouth, ate half, and put the other half into my mouth, which was certainly to me an operation far more loving than agreeable.

"The 'Koos-koo-soo' is made from coarsely ground wheat, and is not unlike sago before it is boiled; and the way it is cooked makes it eat very nice; there appeared to be either honey or sugar boiled with it.

"As soon as the Basha had gone through this interesting operation No. 2, the others plunge their hands in and take up a handful, make it into a ball, and then by a peculiar move put it into the mouth. After looking some time in silent wonder, I thought I could manage to do the same, so I plunged my hand into the basin, took up a lot, and tried the tossing business; but I found I might as well have tried to toss a pancake. I could not get the stuff to form a ball either by squeezing or tossing. I tried to toss it into my mouth, but here I totally failed, for more of it fell on my beard than went into my mouth, which caused considerable laughter all round. I saw I could do nothing that way, and at last had to call in the aid of a spoon, with which I managed comfortably, and soon made up for lost time. After partaking of this for some considerable time, the Basha draws the dish near him, and prepares it to receive the meat, which, with the gravy, is placed on the top, the latter sinking into the 'Koos-koo-soo' makes it absolutely fine. Now was the time to see the Moors eating meat, &c., without knives or forks. They would take up a fowl, pull a piece off with their fingers and put it down again, to be in turn picked up all round until all was gone; and very expert they are too. However, I had eaten sufficiently. I was spared the picking up of any meat after the others. After this course came melons and grapes, and then followed tea, making altogether about as extraordinary a feast as I ever sat down to. But still it was one that clearly showed me that the better class of Moors know how to live well; they are evidently well versed in what is good for comforting the inner man; they never drink anything but water, all are consequently teetotalers.

"After we had finished, the soldiers and workmen set to, and judging from the rapidity of their movements, it was easily seen that most of them had never enjoyed such a banquet in their lives, and consequently they took in an enormous quantity. I must confess, for myself, that I did not eat so much in any one meal while in Morocco as on that occasion."

The address delivered at Tangier:—

"Tangier, 12th of 12th month, 1863.

"Yesterday morning, from the deck of a friendly steamer, I beheld, for the first time, your bright city, quietly lying, as it were, in the lap of your tranquil hills; and I was soon met by the large and active crowd of water-waders, anxious to see and receive their good and able friend and brother, Sir Moses Montefiore, whose companion I am.

"I had not long been landed when I climbed your heights, walked about your walls, and through your gates, visited some of your charming gardens, commanding admirable views, and examined your busy market. Before the day was ended I had enquired of your kind and intelligent citizens respecting other towns of your North-Western African Empire, and also respecting the roads and modes of conveyance by which they may communicate with each other, and send to, or receive from distant countries the productions and manufactures which contribute so much to man's comfort and enjoyment.

"Having no mercantile or selfish object of my own in view, it was a long-felt interest in Africa which was the chief stimulus to my curiosity, and which also suggested on the night or the following morning the thoughts which I may not uselessly lay before you.

"The chief men of Morocco, doubtless, resemble those in similar positions in other countries, in desiring the prosperity of their country, and the welfare of those about them. Men who have but little will also supply but little. Poor subjects can pay but little revenue to their sovereign, and a poor and miserable peasantry do not do well for their lords or themselves. You will say that one so recently come to Tangier must know very little about it. I may answer that he who has just arrived brings fresh eyes, which are struck most forcibly by objects which are unnoticed by eyes which have had them always before them.

"Thanks to smooth water I was safely, as well as quickly, carried through a good part of a mile of low water; but how could merchandise, or most necessary and useful machinery, a hundred times heavier than the heaviest man, be conveyed between the shore and a ship? A *pier* of some kind is an object of absolute necessity, if Tangier is to be a really important commercial city.

"A practiced and observing eye may learn much by a very short inspection of a market, if the objects exposed for sale, and the buyers and sellers, are scrutinized and considered. The people may be numerous, well grown, and active, and their countenances may exhibit an intelligence which their rulers may be well pleased that they possess. If, however, the articles which are offered for sale are neither valuable nor abundant, and the persons and conveyances of those who bring them, and of those who are to be the purchasers are indicative of poverty, the conclusion must be as correct as obvious, that wealth and resources must be deficient, although it may not be impossible that a limited number of men of fortune may be living in the country. Such have been the impressions which I have already received in the market of Tangier.

"In traversing the city in different directions, I have been struck with the cleanness and brightness of the whitewashed walls, and the ways appeared to be much more free from impurities, and better swept, than I had anticipated after what I had observed in other eastern and African cities; but this state was not universal, and in many places the paving needs much repair to make it tolerable for the foot passengers, or suitable for the conveyances which it would be most advantageous to introduce.

"When I surveyed the walls, and examined some portions more closely, I noticed a partial dilapidation and ruin, which attracted my curiosity, and I learned that this was the result of hostile foreign violence, and that it was a memorial of many years standing. It struck me that it was by no means pleasing to keep in view these reminiscences of past aggression and disasters, and that it was equally undesirable to spend money in restoring them as military works, but that it would be at once a gratifying and useful change to make these walls, which are at an elevated and healthful part of the city, a portion of an educational institution, either college or school, founded for the benefit of the youth of the city and its vicinity, and for their instruction in those useful branches of knowledge which may already afford interest, enjoyment, and satisfaction to some of the higher classes, but which, if diffused through all classes of the community, would be favourable to a degree of prosperity and happiness of which their limited and partial influence can afford no idea. On such an institution let it be conspicuously inscribed, 'Knowledge is Power.' 'Virtue is Happiness.'

"Having had the privilege of visiting two important and interesting countries inhabited by your co-religionists — Turkey and Egypt, — it gives me pleasure to remind you of that which you may have seen, and which I have witnessed there.

"In Constantinople, the capital city of Turkey, the diffusion of knowledge is now so much approved and patronized that the Ministers of the Sultan do not think it beneath them to make themselves masters of the sciences, and deliver courses of lectures upon them in the public institutions; and the Sultan himself visits the hospitals, and directs the construction of wards, in which medicine and surgery are taught as well as practised. In Egypt, the ancient fertility of the country watered by the Nile is rivalled, if not equalled, by that which rewards the present cultivators of the soil, whose corn and cotton are sent to distant parts of the world, and are constantly increasing the comforts, the resources, and the credit of the Viceroy, the Pacha, and the people; whilst the useful arts — engineering, navigation, and medicine are encouraged and rewarded. Egypt, in fact, is exhibiting, at the north-eastern extremity of Africa, an example which her sister, Morocco, at the west, would do well to follow and emulate. A prompt reward was never more easily within her reach than at the present time.

"Perhaps you may say, we have powerful neighbours ready and able to take advantage of any opportunity which may favour their appropriating to themselves everything which we inherit from our forefathers. All our energies must be devoted to keeping our own, and we are averse to every change. I, too, love my country; but I trust in the assurance, which I believe that Mohammedans, Israelites, and Christians agree in receiving with comfort and satisfaction, that when one's ways are pleasing to the Almighty, He makes even enemies to be at peace. So Morocco, directing all her resources, moral as well as physical, to internal improvements —amongst which a theoretical and practical reform in her criminal jurisprudence, in accordance with the progress of the age, will form a most important part—and scrupulously avoiding every sustainable ground of offence to all, will afford no handle to her enemies, should she have any, and defended by the Disposer of the Universe will be too much for them to take or injure.

"Transient visitors have been the harbingers of great events; and though this may not be the case in the present instance, do not reject the sincere good wishes of the visitor of a few hours."

THOMAS HODGKIN, M.D.

Notices of some superficial geological appearances I observed in the north-west portion of Morocco, on a visit to Tangier, a coasting voyage to Mogador, a land journey from thence to Morocco, and from that city to Mazagan, and in the voyage thence to Gibraltar by way of Tangier.

On approaching the African coast from Cadiz, we are struck with the magnificent southern pillar of Hercules, now called the "Apes' Mountain," rising from the Straits of Gibraltar, to even a greater height than its northern fellow—the British Rock, which it resembles in some of its characters, and which probably, like it, is composed of an old limestone. Similar hills, but of less elevation, form the African coast till the Bay of Tangier is reached; the flatter, but rich coast of Spain being, meanwhile, distinctly visible on the right.

The Bay of Tangier is nearly equal in depth and breadth. Its bottom and northern sides are bounded by verdant downs.

The noted little city of Tangier, which stands at its entrance, on its southern side, is beautiful and bright at a distance. Reposing on the slope of a hill, green with gardens and trees above and at each side, the city has a very remarkable and picturesque appearance. Its white houses and walls rise gradually, as steps, one above another, and numerous old cannon point from rows of port-holes at different heights.

Quitting the city at its eastern extremity, we come upon several old tan-pits, which seem to have been cut in the native rock. Beyond these, the cliffs, rising from the sandy shore, consist of strata which have been so displaced as to assume a vertical position. They are composed of sandstone, alternating with a schistose rock, which, under the influence of the weather, separates into flaky layers. Thin seams of crystallized carbonate of lime are interposed between some of the vertical strata.

Continuing a course eastward along the shore, the cliffs terminate, and we come to low, moveable sand hills, imperfectly covered with vegetation, and in many places perfectly bare, which, as we further advance, becomes a general character. Walking over this tract is very fatiguing, nevertheless it appears to be traversed by two or three routes, well frequented by foot passengers, as well as by horses, mules, and camels. At the further extremity of the bay the hills are lower than at its mouth, and a passage between them affords a bed to a small river which empties itself into the sea at this place. Very near to its mouth, this stream was crossed by a substantial Roman bridge, the remains of which form a remarkable ruin, admirably represented in the beautiful picture which graced this year's Exhibition, by Cook. Scarcely a mile above this ruin the river is crossed by a modern bridge, very conspicuous from its white colour, which is still in use.

The encroachment on the beautiful and productive face of the country by sand, brought upon it by north-western winds, is a remarkable phenomenon, which, as it must tend to the rapid deterioration of the country, is worthy of special attention; but as it is not confined to this part of the coast, I shall defer the notice of it till I speak of Mogador, where the ravages of this process are still more striking and extensive.

Before quitting the Bay of Tangier I must not omit to mention the reefs of rocks which now uselessly indicate the situation of the moles which at one time gave to Tangier a most necessary and convenient harbour. This work, so essential to commerce and to the protection of life, was destroyed by English orders when the possession of the city was surrendered. There are, probably, no persons who so sensibly feel the inconvenience and danger arising from this destruction as our own countrymen.

Almost immediately after leaving Tangier, we passed Cape Spartel. The coast in this direction consists, for some miles, of undulating hills, for the most part covered with trees and verdure, with a few good country houses near the summits, amongst which those of the British Minister, Sir J. Drummond Hay, and of our late Consul-general, T. F. Reade, are the best and most attractive.

Proceeding southward the coast is flatter, though hills are seen at no great distance inland.

In making our way to Saffi, we stood out to sea during a considerable part of the course, but for several miles before reaching that port, we were sufficiently near to see that cliffs of considerable elevation rise abruptly from the shore. This is not the case at the town of Saffi itself, which is situated on ground gradually rising from the sea; yet there are some rocks in the sea and rather low cliffs on the mainland towards the southern part of the town, which are of a dull red or puce colour, and which I suspect to be composed of sandstone; but the surf was breaking with so much force during the several hours we remained off the town, that I had no opportunity of landing or of approaching near the shore. Between Saffi and Mogador, to which place we directed our course for safer landing, we kept, for prudential reasons, too distant from the coast to admit of my forming an opinion, or giving a description of it.

The town of Mogador is situated in a considerable bay, where the shore is even flatter than at Saffi, though there is rising ground near and behind it.

Mogador Island, which rises to a considerable height, at the distance of about a mile from the mainland, appears chiefly to consist of red sandstone, and several reefs and rocks of the same description are scattered from the shore itself, to some distance in the sea, and being often completely covered by the tide, or just breaking the waves into surf, render landing difficult and dangerous, and frequently impracticable. We remained about a week at Mogador, which afforded a good opportunity of seeing the place.

At Mogador the rocks, and what little there is of cliff, consist of a deep dull red or puce-coloured sandstone. There are some to the left, or north side, of the harbour, whilst to the right, or south side, we see nothing but a flat plain of sand, behind which rise low, bare sand hills, with the Mogador river at the base, which runs to its mouth a mile and a-half or two miles to the right. On the left we have low cliffs, rising some feet above the sea, consisting of the before mentioned sandstone, upon which rests a bed of water-worn stones of various sizes, feebly held together. There is a thin strip of this elevated land running along the coast, where it forms the commencement of the route to Saffi, and proceeding from Mogador towards that place, we have the sea on our left, and on the right low land, which in some places is extensively overflowed with water from the sea.

The destruction of this part of the coast is evidently owing to two causes. Though the sandstone rock affords some resistance to the sea, the larger waves, when they dash against the shingle bed, disintegrate and loosen it, and the action of the north-west wind following upon this disintegration, carries the particles of sand inland, and, as it would seem, not merely the sand which has already formed part of the dry land, but also the sand of the shore, which the sea from time to time is throwing upon it. The transport of this wind-born sand is a phenomenon well worthy of attention, since it is impossible to say to what amount it may bring the sterility of a desert over a fertile country. I was told that a very small and trivial object is sufficient to check the progress of the sand in its eastward course, and form the nucleus of a sand hill, which, if it were permanent, might be covered with vegetation; but it seems this favourable result is generally prevented by a change of wind (though it may be to a very small amount), sweeping away the mound which previous blasts had caused. The prevalence of wind from a western point has the effect of keeping the soil in motion, and chiefly in a similar direction. Nevertheless, the fact that on some of the hills near the coast the white broom abounds, and acquires the height of a shrub, sometimes eight or ten feet, and is not only useful as affording some nourishment to cattle, but also in retarding the encroachments of the sand, suggests it is not improbable that, by the judicious employment of planting and the erection of screens in particular spots, a very beneficial influence might be exerted, not merely in checking the advancing injury, but in really adding to the amount of production already obtained.

It would be a happy application of botanical knowledge to discover and introduce the plants best adapted to answer this purpose. The accumulation of sand is already very considerable. A small palace by the sea-side, built by the Sultan who founded Mogador, is rendered untenable and useless by the sand, which has nearly filled some of the apartments, and raised such a mound on both sides of the enclosing wall, that, although about eighteen feet in height, it may be walked over without a ladder. The sand has also been carried for miles into the interior, forming hills of considerable height, and the road from the city towards Morocco, instead of passing directly towards the Mogador river, now takes a somewhat winding course near to the seashore, and does not come upon the river till some twelve or fourteen miles have been travelled. I cannot refrain from expressing my solicitude that the encroachments of the sand may receive serious attention from the Sultan's Government.

Whilst examining the sandstone rocks which are seen behind the Mogador harbour and the Christian Cemetery, my attention was caught by a thin stratum of limestone, which not only partially covers them, but also penetrates into their fissures and crevices. I could not then comprehend its character; but in the course of the journey from Mogador to the city of Morocco, and from thence to Mazagan, I had indubitable evidence that this covering of limestone is only a small part of a most extensive and remarkable formation, which has covered the greater part of the face of the country traversed by these routes, and doubtless spreading far beyond them. Before I attempt to describe the several peculiarities of character, which I noticed in different localities, and under different circumstances, I believe I shall render myself more intelligible if I anticipate the conclusion at which I arrived after I had had the opportunity of seeing and combining them. There seemed to be no doubt that the formation is due to the deposition of carbonate of lime, for the most part very impure, by water which had held it in solution. Having in this respect some resemblance to the limestone, evidently deposited at a recent period between Rome and Tivoli, and called travertin, I applied this name to the formation in question, as soon as I acquired a notion of its nature; but as it is far less crystalline than most of the Italian travertin, I believe it would be more accurate to regard it as a tufa, though even this would not be universally applicable. More extended observations than I had the opportunity of making may lead to an opinion as to the sources whence the depositing water flowed; but the facts which, having seen, I am about to relate, seem clearly to indicate that it must have risen to a considerable height, having left the deposit on high land, and even on the sides of hills of considerable elevation; and yet that the deposition has been long subsequent to those commotions of the earth's surface by which the older rocks—quartz, schist, old limestone, porphyry, and even granite (though I did not see any of the last-named rock *in situ*), have been brought into something like their present position.

Unequivocal evidences of the course taken by the flowing water may be found in the fragments of older formation, more or less worn by attrition, which it has brought along with it and left by the way, enclosed in its own deposit, or now lying amongst the fragments on its broken surface.

Thus, in advancing from the coast inland, fragments of rocks are found, at first lying small and few, but gradually increasing both in size and number. If, however, we had crossed the region whence some of them were derived, we did not find any of that description beyond it. Although our course lay towards the lofty Atlas range, when I was struck with this interesting fact, I do not believe that we were proceeding exactly in the opposite direction to that which the depositing flood had taken, for although the water-worn fragments of porphyry increased both in size and number, till they almost exclusively formed the mass of these transported materials, they were by no means generally of that description of porphyry of which it might be reasonably conjectured that the nearest portion of the range consisted. Green porphyry was the prevailing rock transported in connection with the deposit, whilst brown, red, and liver-coloured porphyry abounded in the bed of the river Nefis, proceeding from the nearest part of the range. I may now proceed with the description of the facts which I noticed, nearly in the order in which they fell under my observation.

Having forded the Mogador river, and passed between the before-mentioned deserted palace on the right, and the Mohammedan saint's mausoleum on the left, we ascended a little hill, on which a Moorish village stands. It appears to have escaped the pervading sand with which the adjoining country is desolated, and the white broom, in full blossom, was abundant, and perfumed the air. Amongst the numerous loose stones strewed upon the ground, I saw very many which were evidently portions of stalactites of very various sizes, some not larger than a finger, others as big as a leg or thigh. Notwithstanding their stalactitic character, they had not a crystalline appearance. Though I could not at the time account for them, I have now no doubt that they belonged to the extensive deposit of which I have been speaking, and may possibly have been connected with some cavern or fissure when Mogador Island probably formed part of the main land. We had not proceeded much further before it became evident that we were coming on a limestone country; and the rock being to a great extent almost bare, its character was exposed, showing a large, flat reniform surface, in layers, though not crystallized. Large portions appeared undisturbed, at least unbroken; others exhibited cracks with little, if any, displacement. When our course had brought us again to the Mogador river, we found it deeply sunk between precipitous banks, showing the strata of alluvium, resting on the travertin. We forded it at a part where the exposed travertin, or tufa, was several feet in thickness and forming steps. It was composed of rounded pebbles of different kinds, and my notes mention shells also, which, if my recollection serves me, seemed to be bivalves, cemented by the travertin. There were many patches of a light, brightish red, or peach-blossom colour, reminding me of the hard limestones of Sicily and Syria, which are not unfrequently mottled with a similar tinge. Amongst the pebbles I noticed flint chert, or chalcedony, some of which were evidently derived from seams or veins, and also fragments of hematite, which last appeared to me to furnish the colouring matter to the limestone before-mentioned. Fragments of the same description abound in the bed of the stream, and some of the kind, especially cornelians, are found on the sea-shore at Mogador. In the low ground, through which the river passes, the bed of alluvium resting on the travertin is, in many places, of considerable thickness; but on the higher spots the travertin is either as bare as a flagstone pavement, or covered with the numerous loose fragments into which the layers separate when they have, as it were, exfoliated from the beds beneath them. When further decomposed, they appear to furnish a tolerably fertile soil, to make use of which the larger fragments are collected in heaps, or formed into walls, somewhat like those of Oxfordshire and Warwickshire, for protection and division. A few miles beyond the crossing of the Mogador river, the path is over a true limestone formation, and I at first imagined there was an obvious transition from the recent travertin to this older rock; but the idea was soon completely set aside. The strata of the limestone rock were distinctly inclined, and a good opportunity for seeing them was given in the precipitous sides of the course of a stream which, at that time, was nearly dried up. The beds of limestone are of different thickness, and the thickest and strongest, being the most durable, project in distinct ridges. At a particular spot, at which the limestone strata formed steps, a thin layer of the travertin, or tufa, gave a partial, but continuous, cover to these steps, as a piece of carpeting or oil-cloth does to an ordinary staircase, evincing an unequivocal distinction between the two formations. Though the superficial covering of recent formation maintains its general character with little variation through the greater part of our route, we occasionally met with modifications well worthy of notice. The loose stones scattered upon the surface, are not merely the broken fragments of exfoliated layers already mentioned, but in some few instances, and in particular localities, more or less globular masses were found, which did not owe their figure to attrition, but to their original formation, since, when broken, they were found to consist of concentric layers deposited upon a nucleus which, in some cases, is very much softer than the coating layers. In fact they bore a striking resemblance, in point of structure, to some of the calculi formed in the interior of animals. They seem to indicate both the motion of the depositing fluid and the rapidity with which it must have precipitated the earthy matters which it held in solution. I may observe that one of the localities which furnished these specimens was near to our encampment at Ain Oumast. The upper or later layers of the travertin, or tufa formation, are by far the purest, that is to say, the most exempt from included adventitious or foreign substances, and their characters are remarkably uniform throughout the extensive district which they cover. The lower beds, on the contrary, are the most various, both as respects their own character, and as regards the included fragments. In fact, it would seem that the earliest effusion of this calcareous deposit was expended in cementing the very various loose and rounded fragments over which it was poured. Hence the corresponding variety in the fragments scattered over the surface of the ground, wherever the removal of the upper layers has allowed the lower beds of a conglomerate character to be disintegrated. The firm upper layers, if free from cracks, constitute a good roofing, whilst the lower bed of conglomerated pebbles is readily excavated.

Proceeding from Sidi Mokhtar, the route tends towards a group of conical, flat-topped hills, which we had perceived the preceding day at a distance. Fragments of chalcedony, scattered on the ground, attracted our attention. We had seen several of the same description, but they were neither so general nor of such large size as we now found them, the nearer we approached these hills. Many of the masses were a foot or more in diameter, and when fractured, exhibited concentric lines like agates, the colours being greyish white, and something between a mauve and lead colour. I was particularly struck with the apparent freshness of the external surface of a large number of these nodulous masses, evincing that they had been little altered, either by exposure or by attrition. It was particularly remarkable that the external surface was not composed of any investing materials, like the silicate of lime coating the flint nodules found in chalk, the deeper colour being as fresh as upon any part of the interior. Independently of colour, the surface of those masses was by no means of uniform character. In some it was minutely mammilated, and on others there was something of an approach to crystallization. Some masses were nearly or quite solid, whilst others had cavities lined with chalcedony, or, in a few instances, with crystallized quartz, or containing a light cellular silicious material of very inderterminate form. To complete the description of these silicious nodulous masses, which may, perhaps, be considered the most interesting part of my observations, I must give some account of the conical hills, to which I have already alluded.

Our route passed between some of them. They appeared to consist of a white limestone, much resembling chalk, and it was evident that the flat, well defined, almost horizontal, summits were determined by a thick bed of a silicious or cherty character. Other layers of the same description, and parallel to it, might, in some cases be seen lower down the hill.

Where the uppermost layers had been wholly removed, the table-like form was lost, so that the lower hills were distinguished by their rounded summits. On our journey to Morocco, I had no opportunity of going up to any of these hills, but I found fragments of the limestone, which appeared to have come from them, which somewhat resembled the hard chalk in the neighbourhood of the Giant's Causeway.

There are indications of flint veins of different colours and various thickness; but I could find nothing like the flint nodules embedded in its matrix. On our returning route, after passing the Jiblet Hills, we again crossed a tract abounding with chalcedonic nodules and, though we saw no flat-topped, conical hills, there were many of the lower rounded character resulting from them. Our resting place at Smira was not far from one of these reduced hills, and I took the opportunity of exploring it. The side by which we had passed had, from some cause, been removed, forming a low cliff, exposing not only a section of the limestone, but also a layer of the travertin resting upon it. Impressed with the idea that the nodules, like the flint layers, had been formed in the limestone, I perseveringly sought for them *in situ*, but although numbers were lying on the ground, I could not find a single one in the limestone cliff, yet I found one or more specimens embedded in the undisturbed conglomerate bed beneath the upper layer of travertin. I had no conception of their having been formed subsequently to the disintegration of the limestone until my return to England, when I showed the specimens which I brought with me to my friend, Wm. Pengelly, who immediately recognised them as beekites. He subsequently sent me a copy of his paper, in which the Devonshire beekites, and the conglomerate bed in which they are found, are minutely described, and on reading it I perceived the reason of my search for the nodulous chalcedony in the undisturbed limestone having been in vain. There seems, however, to be a marked difference between the beekites of Devonshire and those of Morocco.* The former, as described in my friend's paper, would seem to be formed by a process investing a nucleus of so frail a character as frequently to leave a cavity produced by its decay.

---

* Since sending the paper to Bath, I have seen specimens of the Devonshire beekites, brought by W. Pengelly, and have found them *in situ* at Paignton. They differ considerably from those of Morocco, but fully confirm the statements which I have here made.

Such is apparently the case with some of the smaller globular beekites of Morocco; but most of the larger, and very many of the smaller, have a decidedly stalactitic character, and one of the small specimens which I brought home with me exhibits the silicious matter so formed upon a fragment of the hard limestone, accounting at once for the absence of any coating of silicate of lime, and for the freshness of surface so remarkable a character of the silicious masses when dislodged from the bed in which they had been contained. If I offer a conjecture as to the process by which these concretions of silex have been formed it would be, that a very large tract of a limestone formation, somewhat resembling chalk, has been broken up, leaving, at intervals, those portions which we now see as table-topped and round-topped hills, somewhat like the cones of earth left by our excavators to indicate the amount of work which they have performed. That this limestone abounded in silicious matter is evident from the thick layers of flint, petrosilex, or chert, conspicuous in some of these hills, not merely near their summits, determining their curious forms, but also near the base. The process of solution and segregation being continued, or renewed in the vast quantity of disturbed limestone, seems to have allowed of its deposition in the cavities left between the broken fragments. Beekites are therefore there found under the two forms which I have noticed. I may observe that for about half-a-mile, in which I traced the travertin in close proximity to the undisturbed limestone rock near Smira, I remarked a layer of crystallized carbonate of lime in the form called dog's-tooth spar, which formed a continuous horizontal line.

Although I could find none of the chalcedonic masses, which must be called beckites, in the limestone or hard chalk, I saw, near Smira (the only locality in which I could really examine this formation *in situ*), besides the thick continuous layers of flint or chert, detached masses of similar composition, which, though detached, were arranged horizontally. Some of these decidedly approached the flat rounded form seen in some specimens of Menilite and Egyptian jasper. The limestone matrix was here gritty, as if mixed with fine sand.

I have repeatedly alluded to the conglomerate bed, by which term I wish to designate the under portion of the travertin, or tufa, covering so large a portion of the face of the country. It will be borne in mind that this bed is not universally present, as the firmer portion, having the character of rock, or stone, not unfrequently rests immediately upon the solid older rock, whether limestone, schist, or quartz; but when present, along with the firmer travertin, the conglomerate is the lower. It is not uniform in its character, differing, as I have described, in the foreign materials which it encloses. It also differs in the characters proper to itself as to firmness, composition, and colour. In one district the peculiarity was sufficiently remarkable to claim a short description.

At the camping place of Minzala Emzody, by the side of a small, but most valuable stream, the neighbouring ground, chiefly to the east, rises in low hills or downs of a remarkably white colour, and as far as my opportunity of observation allowed me to ascertain, they consisted chiefly of what may be regarded as the upper portion of a deep conglomerate bed. The lower portion was full of water-worn fragments of porphyry, chiefly green, and pebbles of the same kind are scattered through the upper portion also. The striking peculiarity of this upper portion is its great tendency to disintegration, readily crumbling to pieces, part becoming a softish powder, which might easily be diffused through water as white-wash, whilst the other portion remains in irregular roundish nodules, from the size of horse beans upwards. Suspecting that they might be portions of some different and distantly formed mineral, I broke several of them; but they seemed universally to consist of the travertin itself, very considerably indurated, and on carefully examining the fresh fracture of a good specimen, I noticed a multitude of minute specks producing a greyish colour. They glistened a little, and as far as I could ascertain on the spot consisted of very minute granules of silex, deposited in small cavities, such as would be left between two concave surfaces, both concavities being turned the same way, and the larger being inwards. Water seems freely to filter through this travertin, and the stream by the encampment issues from pits, which have been sunk in it, about a quarter of a mile above.

It is probable that many of the wells which we passed in the course of our journey derived their water from the conglomerate bed, but we made no special inquiry on this point, yet I cannot omit to mention that between Minzala Emzody and the city of Morocco we were induced to halt for refreshment beside a well, carefully provided with some rude apparatus for drawing the water by means of a roller, the ends of which were supported upon two forked sticks fixed on the wall. The rope and roller were wanting; but the ingenuity of Captain Armytage quickly supplied the deficiency by combining several pieces of the native cordage which we had with us. However, when the water was drawn up from a considerable depth, it was found to be cold, clear, and good in appearance; but with a very decided sulphurous odour like that of St. Barnard's Well, near Leith. This, fact is not without interest in connection with the travertin formation

From the account which I have already given it will be evident that, either by the removal of the travertin, or from the depositing flood not having reached a sufficient elevation, the older rocks are partially exposed within the district in which the travertin prevails. Thus, at no great distance from Mogador, the much older limestone is exposed. Near Minzala Emzody we had the opportunity of seeing a very different class of rocks.

In the very extensive valley lying between the long Atlas range and the much lower range, called the Jiblet Hills, in which the city of Morocco is situated, comparatively isolated elevations forming single hills, or small groups arise, more especially near the foot of the smaller range. A remarkable group of seven hills rises more distinctly from the plain, not far from the city. Amongst the polite and kind attentions shewn by the Sultan to Sir Moses Montefiore and his party were his directions that some of them, including myself, should be conducted to a large, enclosed, and well-kept Imperial estate, consisting of fields, olive and orange orchards, a very large tank, or artificial lake, and courses of water. It was presumed to be frequented by game, and my companions, besides having their guns, were accompanied by greyhounds, sent by the Sultan for their amusement. Whilst my friends were engaged with these pursuits I took advantage of the occasion to ride, with one of the soldiers, towards the group of hills before mentioned, which is not far distant. We passed over cultivated fields, and tracts of bare travertin, towards a path at the foot of the nearest hill. I observed, at some distance up its side, a Mahometan saint's tomb, or sacred house, of large size, and, by the soldier's signs, I perceived that he regarded it with reverence, and objected to my approaching it. I wished neither to offend him nor to abandon my curiosity, and quietly persisted, changing my course a little, so as to avoid tending to the path leading up to the building, which, for the time, suspended opposition, till coming almost to the foot of the hill, the soldier stopped, and I went a little further to enable me to see some of the masses of stone which had fallen from the hill side, which is here precipitous, and rocky at the upper part, with an inclined plain at the base, formed by the débris. I obtained a fragment, by which I learnt that the rock is a remarkably dark coloured, and in some portions almost black marble, so hard as in parts scarcely to be scratched with a knife. It was of the same kind with much of the stone to be seen in the city, where, in former times, it has been used in paving and building; and, as applied to these purposes, I had repeated opportunities of seeing its capacity for polish, and its remarkable mottled appearance. The form of the exposed rock on the side of the hill is also worthy of notice. It exhibits tiers of oblong-square surfaces, nearly, or quite upright, with the upper angles rounded off.

As our returning route was across the Jiblet range, I had an opportunity of seeing some of its component rocks at its base, and in the path through which we went. Notwithstanding the evidence that there was granite in the vicinity, I saw none of it *in situ*.

Shortly after crossing the ford of the river Tensift, about five miles from Morocco, we came upon the gently inclined, but undulating plain, at the foot of the hills. I observed at some distance to the right the appearance of white buildings, which, as we came nearer, seemed to be huge masses of hewn stone taken from a quarry, and, leaving the company for a mile or more, I went up to them, when, to my surprise, I found they consisted of blocks of pure white compact quartz, being part of a vein, or dyke, of this substance, which could not be less than sixteen feet across. The ground for some distance around was whitened by innumerable fragments of the same material. Notwithstanding the unquestionable hardness, and apparent durability of the masses of quartz rock at this spot, and in others which we met with in crossing the Jiblet range, the general tendency to disintegration of the quartz veins is very remarkable, the ground being rendered as white as chalk by the fragments covering it, where the veins crop out. I frequently looked for indications of gold in the different situations in which quartz occurred, but neither with the naked eye nor with a lense did I ever perceive the smallest particle. The quartz veins and dykes are in schist; schistose rocks in several varieties of form and colour being the prevailing constituent of this range, so far as we could observe it. In many places the beds have their layers in a more or less vertical position, and the travertin is found immediately applied to the exposed extremities of the laminæ. Fissures and cracks are, for the most part, so numerous as to render the schist inapplicable to any of the ordinary purposes of building; but my friend, Consul-General T. F. Reade, found in one situation, slate of a character quite suitable for the roofing of buildings.

I must not omit the following very important letter which my valued friend, Sir Moses Montefiore, addressed to the Jews of Morocco, in the month of September, 1864, after our return home.

EAST CLIFF LODGE, RAMSGATE,

6th *Elul.*—7th *September*, 5624—1864.

To the RABBIS, ELDERS, AND CONGREGATIONAL AUTHORITIES

OF THE JEWS OF MOROCCO.

MY DEAR BRETHREN AND FRIENDS,

Throughout the world, a chief characteristic of the Jews is that of being loyal, obedient, and peaceful subjects of their sovereign. From what I have seen and know of my brethren in Morocco, I feel assured they are not exceptions to this universally admitted truth. The precepts inculcating this conduct are enforced on us by the Sacred Scriptures, and by the wise exhortations of our sages.

Unless due respect be paid to the just exercise of legally constituted authority, there can be neither order nor safety. Happily, the Imperial Edict of your August Sovereign is intended to sustain the cause of justice and humanity throughout the Moorish Empire; and though it may be that in some places the subordinate authorities abuse the powers with which they are entrusted, let it not be said that their severity or wrong doing is attributable to any manifestation of disrespect on your part. You must never for a moment forget the loyalty, the affection, and respect due to your Sovereign, on whom you must rely, and to whom, in case of need, you must appeal for protection against oppression and redress for injury.

Let neither actions nor words from you induce your fellow-countrymen of the Mahommedan faith to suppose that you are in any way unmindful or regardless of your duties as subjects of His Imperial Majesty; but on the contrary, that it is your ardent desire, and most anxious wish, to testify your love and obedience towards him, and also to cultivate the esteem and good-will of your fellow-countrymen.

It is by conduct such as this we may hope that, under the Almighty's blessing, the hearts of those who would molest or injure you will be softened, or that should injustice be done it will be speedily and surely punished.

Most ardently and most anxiously do I desire your welfare. To promote this I have laboured with intense anxiety. I know full well, that these my words are conveyed to willing listeners—to those who fully recognise their truth; and I feel sure that you will, to the utmost of your ability, seek to give effect to my wishes.

Over the poorer and less educated classes of our brethren in Morocco, let your watchful care be exercised so far as in you lies, so that they pay due obedience and respect to the constituted authorities; let them be patient under small annoyances, but firm and reliant on their august sovereign, who will not fail to punish those who abuse his commands, disregard his edict, or venture to inflict serious wrong upon his Jewish subjects.

I trust and believe, that in such cases the ear of your august sovereign will ever be open to your cry.

May it be the will of God to remove from you all further suffering, to inspire your rulers with a spirit of humanity and justice, and to grant to your august sovereign a long and happy reign.

This is the heartfelt prayer of,

Yours faithfully,

MOSES MONTEFIORE.

Before concluding this volume, I wish to mention a testimonial presented to Sir Moses Montefiore by several hundreds of the most influential Jews in Italy, Morocco, and other parts of the world, in order not merely to testify the high esteem they entertained for him personally, but to acknowledge as well the incalculable benefits which the Israelitish people have received from his unwearied zeal in ameliorating the condition of his co-religionists. Nor has Sir Moses been exclusive in his charitable exertions; the whole body of Christians, of every sect and every denomination, has directly or indirectly participated in the innumerable kindnesses his practical benevolence has from time to time in Europe, in Asia, and in Africa unselfishly exercised.

The Testimonial Volume alluded to was bound in Vienna, and is, perhaps, the most elaborate, costly, and beautiful specimen of the art that has ever been executed, alike worthy the subscribers and the recipient. The cover is of royal blue velvet; the heraldic arms of Sir Moses are placed in the centre; allegorical figures on a white ground form each corner; between the corners, at the top and bottom, are flowers in exquisite Mosaic work, the same embellishment running on either side of the heraldic emblem. The whole setting is of the purest gold, and is enriched with a considerable number of precious stones.

The volume contains complimentary addresses, to which the autographs of the various subscribers are added.

THE END.

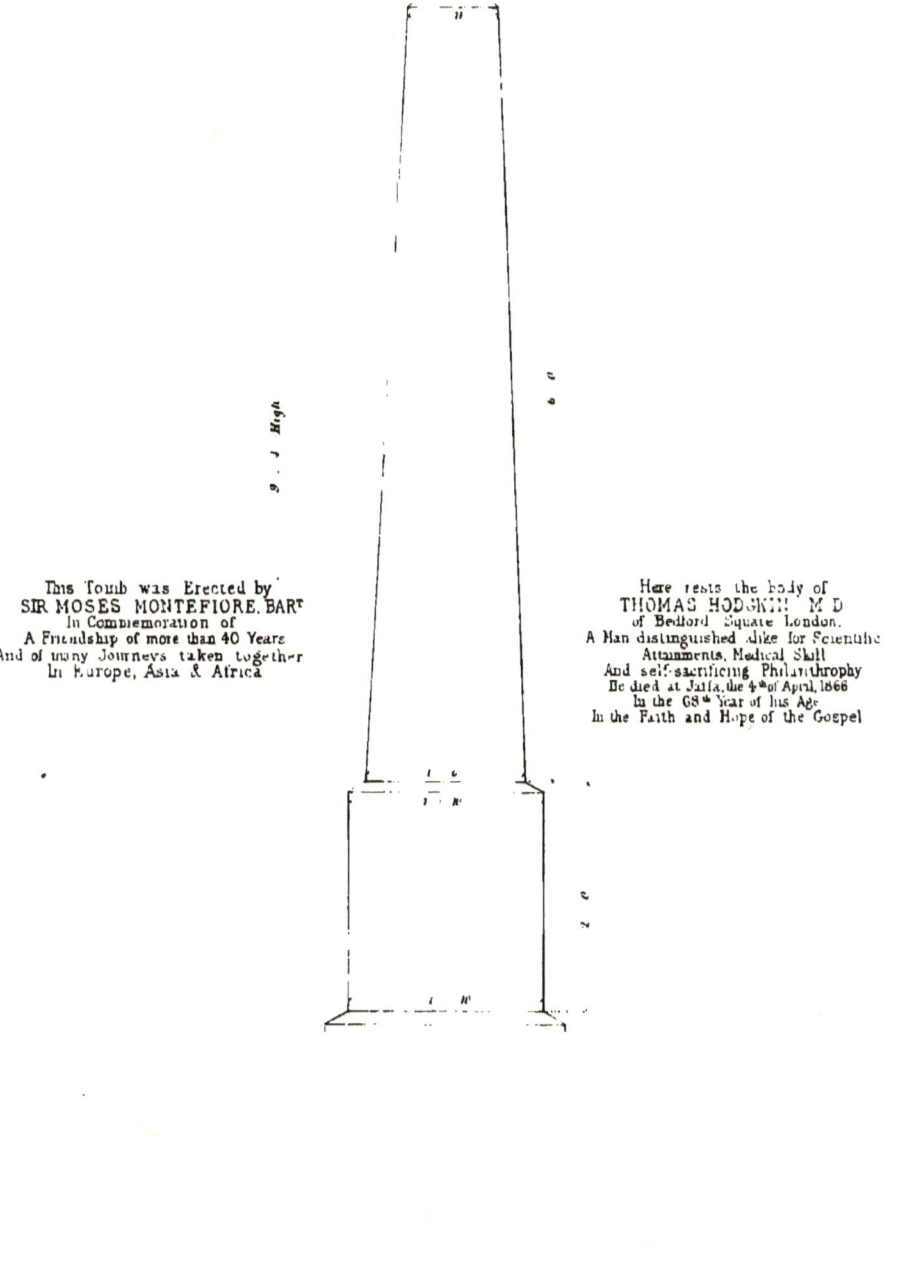

This Tomb was Erected by
SIR MOSES MONTEFIORE, BART
In Commemoration of
A Friendship of more than 40 Years
And of many Journeys taken together
In Europe, Asia & Africa

Here rests the body of
THOMAS HODGKIN M D
of Bedford Square London.
A Man distinguished alike for Scientific
Attainments, Medical Skill
And self-sacrificing Philanthrophy
He died at Jaffa, the 4th of April, 1866
In the 68th Year of his Age
In the Faith and Hope of the Gospel

Mr. Newby's New Publications.

30, WELBECK STREET, CAVENDISH SQUARE.

In Demy 8vo., price 14s. (In the Press).

HISTORY OF IRISH PERIODICAL LITERATURE,

BY

RICHARD ROBERT MADDEN, M.R.I.A.,

Author of "Travels in the East," "Lives and Times of the United Irishmen," "Travels in Turkey, Egypt, Nubia, and Palestine," "Memoirs and Correspondence of the Countess of Blessington," &c., &c., &c.

This History of Irish Periodical Literature, the result of arduous labour and research for the past five years, is not a mere catalogue of names, dates, and compendious characteristics of newspapers and magazines, gleaned from published lists, or memoranda furnished by literary men; but an original and extensive Treatise, illustrative, as it professes to be, of the origin, scope, progress, and design of newspapers, magazines, and periodical miscellanies of all kinds worthy of notice, that have been published in Ireland from the latter part of the seventeenth, to the middle of the nineteenth century.

The importance of such a work, executed with due care, diligence, truthfulness, and impartiality, must be obvious to all by whom reliable knowledge is desired, of contingencies, conjunctures, and controversies on subjects of great pith and moment, that have engaged public attention in Ireland during a period of nearly two centuries.

It abounds with periodical notices of Irish periodical originators, contributors, and editors, remarkable for their position, influence, ability, or eccentricity, of past or recent times.

In 1 Vol. (In the Press).

THE SPAS

OF BELGIUM, GERMANY, SWITZERLAND, FRANCE, AND ITALY,

A Hand-book of the principal Watering Places on the Continent.

BY THOMAS MORE MADDEN, M.D., M.R.I.A.,

Author of "Change of Climate in Pursuit of Health," "The Climate of Malaga," &c.

In 2 Vols., post 8vo., price 21s. (In the Press).

SOME NAMES OF NOBLE NOTE,

BY W. DAVENPORT ADAMS,

Author of "Memorable Battles in English History," "Anecdotal Memoirs of English Princes," &c., &c., &c.

In 1 Vol. Price 12s.

ON CHANGE OF CLIMATE,

A GUIDE FOR TRAVELLERS IN PURSUIT OF HEALTH,

BY THOMAS MORE MADDEN, M.D., M.R.C.S. ENG.

Illustrative of the Advantages of the various localities resorted to by Invalids, for the cure or alleviation of chronic diseases, especially consumption. With Observations on Climate, and its Influences on Health and Disease, the result of extensive personal experience of many Southern Climes,

SPAIN, PORTUGAL, ALGERIA, MOROCCO, FRANCE, ITALY, THE MEDITERRANEAN ISLANDS, EGYPT, &c.

"Dr. Madden has been to most of the places he describes, and his book contains the advantage of a guide, with the personal experience of a traveller. To persons who have determined that they ought to have a change of climate, we can recommend Dr. Madden as a guide."—ATHENÆUM.

"It contains much valuable information respecting various favorite places of resort, and is evidently the work of a well-informed physician."—LANCET.

"Dr. Madden's book deserves confidence—a most accurate and excellent work."— DUBLIN MEDICAL REVIEW.

"It cannot but be of much service to such persons as propose leaving home in search of recreation, or a more benign atmosphere. The Doctor's observations relate to the favorite haunts of English invalids. He criticises each place *seriatim* in every point of view."—READER.

"We strongly advise all those who are going abroad for health's sake to provide themselves with this book. They will find the author in these pages an agreeable gossiping companion as well as a professional adviser, who anticipates most of their difficulties."—DUBLIN EVENING MAIL.

"To the medical profession this book will be invaluable, and to those in ill-health it will be even more desirable, for it will be found not merely a guide for change of climate, but a most interesting volume of travel."—GLOBE.

"Dr. Madden is better qualified to give an opinion as to the salubrity of the places most frequented by invalids than the majority of writers on the subject."—LIVERPOOL ALBION.

"There is something, and a great deal too, for almost every reader in this volume, for the physician, for the invalid, for the historian, for the antiquarian, and for the man of letters. Dr. Madden has rendered a necessary service to the profession and to the public upon the subject under notice."—DUBLIN EVENING POST.

"Dr Madden's work is fraught with instruction that must prove useful both to practitioner and patients who study it."—SANDERS' NEWS LETTER.

"Dr. Madden deserves the thanks of all those persons afflicted with that dire disease, consumption—as well as of those who suffer from chronic bronchitis, asthma, &c. It is the best work on change of climate that has ever been presented to the public."— DAILY POST.

In 2 Volumes, Octavo, price 21s.

ENGLISH AMERICA IN 1862;

OR

PICTURES OF CANADIAN PLACES AND PEOPLE.

EXHIBITING OUR COLONIAL POSSESSIONS ON THE AMERICAN CONTINENT

IN THEIR MORAL, SOCIAL, RELIGIOUS,

PHYSICAL, MILITARY, ECONOMICAL, AND INDUSTRIAL ASPECTS.

By SAMUEL PHILLIPS DAY,

Special Correspondent, in Canada, of the MORNING HERALD.

Author of "Down South; or Experiences at the Seat of War in America," &c., &c.

In 1 Vol., Post 8vo., Price 10s. 6d.

HEROIC IDYLS,

AND OTHER POEMS,

By WALTER SAVAGE LANDOR.

"These Idyls may take their place with those heretofore given us by Mr. Landor. Judged of simply by their merits, they compel that rare admiration which we yield only to noble ideals made palpable by true heart. As recent works they claim the tribute of our wonder, no less than of our delight."—ATHENÆUM.

"The same classical feeling which has given a harmony even to the most fanciful of his 'Imaginary Conversations,' and moulded the thoughts of an English poet in the lines of Greek simplicity and beauty, is to be found here, as delicately marked as ever. Few artists of modern times have taken a larger range, or have carried out a clearly conceived purpose with a steadier hand. When Mr. Landor is gone, we shall have lost at once the founder, and almost the only follower of a peculiar and grand school."—SATURDAY REVIEW.

"Here we recognise the dignified pathos and tranquil beauty characteristic of the best of his 'Hellenics.'"—READER.

"Mr. Landor's works, stamped, as they are, with the impress of high and original intellect, will ensure for him a proud position among the master minds of the period."—BELL's MESSENGER.

"Passages full of vigorous and tender expression, and containing sentiments and thoughts in accordance with the former works of the poet."—OBSERVER.

"A book of rare merit, containing many passages of singular power, grace, and freshness of style, which it would be hard to match in any modern versifier."—MORNING HERALD.

In 1 Vol. Price 5s.

THE BRIDE OF ROUGEMONT,
AND OTHER POEMS,
BY HENRY J. VERLANDER, B.A.,
Author of "The Vestal," &c.

"Forms a very agreeable addition to the stock of modern poetry."—OBSERVER.
"The scenery and accessories are cleverly painted."—LONDON REVIEW.
"Mr. Verlander's muse is one who loves to dwell on the past, and does it with much success."—SUSSEX ADVERTISER.

In 2 Vols., post 8vo., price 21s.

ANECDOTAL MEMOIRS OF ENGLISH PRINCES,
BY W H. DAVENPORT ADAMS,
Author of "Memorable Battles in English History," &c.

"There can be very little doubt of these memoirs being favourably received by the public."—OBSERVER.

"Mr. Adams manifests the same tact and discretion which have made his former publications so highly interesting."—BELL'S MESSENGER.

"The book will interest the general reader and furnish landmarks for the guidance of the student."—MORNING POST.

"Mr Adams has here opened an almost inexhaustible mine of anecdotal wealth. Scattered over the pages of our history anecdotes of the doings of English Princes have hitherto been interesting only, or chiefly, in connection with the era in which the incidents occurred. Mr. Adams has shown that the anecdotes have an interest of their own, apart from their historical connection."—MORNING HERALD.

THE FOURTH EDITION, ILLUSTRATED.
In 1 Vol., post 8vo., price 7s. 6d.

A NARRATIVE OF ADVENTURES IN FRANCE AND FLANDERS,
DURING THE LATE WAR,
BY CAPTAIN EDWARD BOYS,
ROYAL NAVY.

"Readers will like this curious narrative, which has all the charm of truthfulness, which few writers, excepting De Foe, could have written half so truthfully; and Captain Boys' interesting and patriotic story is all truth in itself."—ILLUSTRATED TIMES.

"Many of the events recorded have long since become matters of history; they are, however, so mixed up with personal adventures simple truth conveyed in a simple form, that we read on with unflagging attention."—MORNING ADVERTISER.

"Every youth in Her Majesty's dominions should read these adventures."—DAILY POST.

In 2 Vols., 21s.

IL PELLEGRINO;
OR,
WANDERINGS AND WONDERINGS,
BY CAPTAIN CLAYTON, F.R.G.S., F.S.A.
Author of "Ubique."

"To read Captain Clayton's book without hilarity would be impossible to the gloomiest of home-keeping hermits."—ATHENÆUM.

"A more lively, racy, rollicking 'pilgrim' than Captain Clayton, it has not been our good fortune to meet for a long time."—NEW MONTHLY (July).

"The reader is somehow so led on and on by the spirit of the book, that the end is reached almost unawares, and 'Il Pellegrino,' left with a sigh."—GLOBE.

"The work is extremely pleasant, chatty, and agreeable."—MORNING ADVERTISER.

"'Il Pellegrino' displays alternate humour and sensible reflections."—COURT JOURNAL.

"The author was a most thoughtful reasoner on what he observed."—OBSERVER.

"The author is a frank, outspeaking gentleman, and the reader will accompany him in his peregrinations with pleasure, whilst those who are going abroad will thank him for the information he affords, and which serves to prepare them for what they will meet with in their travels."—NEWS OF THE WORLD.

Price 2s. 6d., beautifully illustrated.

THE HAPPY COTTAGE,
A TALE OF SUMMER'S SUNSHINE,
By the Author of "Kate Vernon," "Agnes Waring."

In 1 Vol., 7s. 6d.

ON SEX IN THE WORLD TO COME,
BY THE REV. G. HOUGHTON A.M.

"A peculiar subject; but a subject of great interest; and in this volume is treated in a masterly style. The language is surpassingly good, showing the author to be a learned and thoughtful man."—NEW QUARTERLY REVIEW.

Second Edition, now ready, in 3 Vols., price 42s.

THE LITERARY LIFE AND CORRESPONDENCE
OF THE
COUNTESS OF BLESSINGTON,
BY R. MADDEN, ESQ., F.R.C.S. ENG.
Author of "Travels in the East," "Life of Savonarola," &c.

"We may, with perfect truth, affirm that during the last fifty years there has been no book of such peculiar interest to the literary and political world. It has contributions from every person of literary reputation—Byron, Sir E. Bulwer, who contributes an original Poem, James, D'Israeli, Maryatt, Savage Landor, Campbell, L. E. L., the Smiths, Shelley, Jenkyn, Sir W. Gell, Jekyll, &c., &c.; as well as letters from the most eminent Statesmen and Foreigners of distinction, the Duke of Wellington, Marquis Wellesley, Marquis Douro, Lords Lyndhurst, Brougham, Durham, Abinger, &c."
—MORNING POST.

In 1 Vol., post 8vo., price 10s. 6d.

OUR PLAGUE SPOT.

In connection with our Policy and Usages as regards Women, our Soldiery, and the Indian Empire.

In 1 Vol., price 7s. 6d.

TAORMINA AND OTHER POEMS.

"It is written with a rare mixture of spirit and grace, and bears the marks of a highly cultivated mind, enriched by travel and by classic lore."—SCOTSMAN.

In 1 Vol., price 2s. 6d.

DRAWING-ROOM CHARADES FOR ACTING,

By C. WARREN ADAMS, Esq.

"A valuable addition to Christmas diversions. It consists of a number of well-constructed scenes for charades."—GUARDIAN.

In 1 Vol., post 8vo., plates, price 10s. 6d.

DEAFNESS AND DISEASES OF THE EAR;

The Fallacies of present treatment exposed and Remedies suggested from the experience of half-a-century,

By W. WRIGHT, Esq.,

Surgeon Aurist (by Royal Sign Manual), to Her Majesty the late Queen Charlotte, &c.

In 1 Vol., price 5s.

FISHES AND FISHING,

By W. WRIGHT, Esq.

"Anglers will find it worth their while to profit by the author's experience."—ATHENÆUM.

"The pages abound in a variety of interesting anecdotes connected with the rod and the line. The work will be found both useful and entertaining to the lovers of the piscatory art."—MORNING POST.

In 1 Vol. 14s.

THE AGE OF PITT AND FOX,

By the Author of "Ireland and its Rulers."

The TIMES says: "We may safely pronounce it to be the best text book that we have yet seen of the age which it professes to describe."

"It is a noble work."—QUARTERLY REVIEW.

"It is a powerful piece of writing."—SPECTATOR.

In 1 Vol., £1 1s., Second Edition.

ILLUSTRATED WITH FIFTY-FOUR SUBJECTS BY

GEORGE SCHARF, JUNR.

THE MANNERS AND CUSTOMS OF THE GREEKS.

By THEODORE PANOFKA

(OF BERLIN).

The TIMES says: "This new publication may be added to a series of works which honorably characterize the present age, infusing a knowledge of things into a branch of learning which too often consisted of a knowledge of mere words, and furnishing the general student with information which was once exclusively confined to the professed archæologist. As a last commendation to this elegant book, let us add that it touches on no point that can exclude it from the hands of youth."

"It will excellently prepare the student for the uses of the vases in the British Museum."—SPECTATOR.

"Great pains, fine taste, and large expense are evident. It does infinite credit to the enterprising publisher."—LITERARY GAZETTE.

In 1 Vol., price 5s.

KNIGHTS OF THE CROSS,

By MRS. AGAR.

"Nothing can be more appropriate than this little volume, from which the young will learn how their forefathers venerated and fought to preserve those places hallowed by the presence of the Saviour."—GUARDIAN.

"Mrs. Agar has written a book which young and old may read with profit and pleasure."—SUNDAY TIMES.

"It is a work of care and research, which parents may well wish to see in the hands of their children."—LEADER.

"A well written history of the Crusades, pleasant to read and good to look upon."—CRITIC.

In 3 Vols., demy 8vo. £2 2s.

THE HISTORY OF THE PAPAL STATES,

By JOHN MILEY, D.D.,

Author of "Rome under Paganism and the Popes."

"Dr. Miley supports his position with a plenitude and profundity of learning, a force and massive power of reasoning, a perspicuity of logical prowess, and a felicity of illustration rarely met in combined existence amongst historians of any age."—MORNING POST.

"Illustrated by profound learning, deep thought, refined taste, and great sagacity."—DUBLIN REVIEW.

"We have no hesitation in recommending these volumes as characterized by learning, eloquence, and original research."—DAILY NEWS.

In 1 Vol. 10s. 6d.
A HISTORY OF THE KINGS OF JUDAH,
By LADY CHATTERTON.

"No Protestant family should be without this excellent work."—NEW QUARTERLY REVIEW.

In 1 Vol., demy 8vo., price 12s.
THE SPORTSMAN'S FRIEND IN A FROST,
By HARRY HIEOVER.

"Harry Hieover's practical knowledge and long experience in field sports render his writings ever amusing and instructive. He relates most pleasing anecdotes of flood and field, and is well worthy of study."—THE FIELD.

"There is amusement as well as intelligence in Harry Hieover's book."—ATHENÆUM.

In 1 Vol., price 5s.
THE SPORTING WORLD,
By HARRY HIEOVER.

"Reading Harry Hieover's book is like listening lazily and luxuriously after dinner to a quiet, gentlemanlike, clever talker."—ATHENÆUM.

"It will be perused with pleasure by all who take an interest in the manly games of our fatherland. It ought to be added to every sportsman's library."—SPORTING REVIEW.

Fourth Edition. Price 2s. 6d.
THE PROPER CONDITION OF ALL HORSES,
By HARRY HIEOVER.

"It should be in the hands of all owners of horses."—BELL'S LIFE.

"A work which every owner of a horse will do well to consult."—MORNING HERALD.

"Every man who is about purchasing a horse, whether it be hunter, riding-horse, lady's palfrey, or cart horse, will do well to make himself acquainted with the contents of this book."—SPORTING MAGAZINE.

In 1 Vol., demy 8vo., price 12s.
SPORTING FACTS AND SPORTING FANCIES,
By HARRY HIEOVER,

Author of "Stable Talk and Table Talk," "The Pocket and the Stud," "The Hunting Field," &c.

"This work will make a valuable and interesting addition to the sportsman's library."—BELL'S LIFE.

"In addition to the immense mass of practical and useful information with which this work abounds, there is a refreshing buoyance and dash about the style, which makes it as attractive and fascinating as the pages of the renowned Nimrod himself."—DISPATCH.

In 1 Vol., price 5s.
HINTS TO HORSEMEN,
SHOWING HOW TO MAKE MONEY BY HORSES,
By HARRY HIEOVER.

"When Harry Hieover gives hints to Horsemen, he does not mean by that term riders exclusively, but owners, breeders, buyers, sellers, and admirers of horses. To teach such men how to make money is to impart no valueless instruction to a large class of mankind. The advice is frankly given, and if no benefit result, it will not be for the want of good counsel."—ATHENÆUM.

"It is by far the most useful and practical book that Harry Hieover has written."—EXPRESS.

In 1 Vol., price 10s. 6d.
GHOST STORIES,
By CATHERINE CROWE,
Author of "Night Side of Nature."

"Mrs. Crowe's volume will delight the lovers of the supernatural, and their name is legion."—MORNING POST.

"These tales are calculated to excite all the feelings of awe, and we may say of terror, with which Ghost Stories have ever been read."—MORNING ADVERTISER.

In 1 Vol., post 8vo., price 5s.
SPIRITUALISM AND THE AGE WE LIVE IN,
By MRS. CROWE,
Author of "Night Side of Nature," "Ghost Stories," &c.

In 1 Vol., 10s. 6d.
SKETCHES FROM NATURE AND JOTTINGS FROM BOOKS,
By W. H. C. NATION,
Author of "Cypress Leaves," "Trifles."

"The author treats of a variety of subjects connected with the manners and habits of modern life in a humourous spirit."—LONDON REVIEW.

In 2 Vols. £1 1s. cloth.

THE LIFE OF PERCY BYSSHE SHELLEY,

By CAPTAIN MEDWIN,

Author of "Conversations with Lord Byron."

"This book must be read by every one interested in literature."—MORNING POST.

"A complete life of Shelley was a desideratum in literature, and there was no man so competent as Captain Medwin to supply it."—INQUIRER.

"The book is sure of exciting much discussion."—LITERARY GAZETTE.

In 1 Vol., 8vo.

A HISTORY OF THE MODERN MUSIC OF WESTERN EUROPE,

FROM THE FIRST CENTURY OF THE CHRISTIAN ERA TO THE PRESENT DAY,

WITH EXAMPLES AND AN APPENDIX EXPLANATORY OF THE THEORY OF THE ANCIENT GREEK MUSIC,

By G. R. KIESWITTER;

With Notes by R. MULLER.

"Herr Kieswitter writes clearly because he sees clearly."—ATHENÆUM.

In 1 Vol. Price 1s. 6d. 10th Edition.

THE FIRST LATIN COURSE,

By REV. J. ARNOLD.

"For beginners, this Latin Grammar is unequalled."—SCHOLASTIC.

In 1 Vol. 5s. Second Edition.

THE ROCK OF ROME,

By THE LATE J. SHERIDAN KNOWLES,

Author of "Virginia," &c.

"Mr. Knowles appears to be only a believer in his Bible, as he comes forward in this work with an earnestness which all true-hearted men will appreciate."—EXAMINER.

"It is a vivid and eloquent exposure of the lofty pretensions of the Church of Rome."—MORNING HERALD.

"It should be in the libraries of all Protestants."—MORNING POST.

In 3 Vols. Price £2 14s.

A CATHOLIC HISTORY OF ENGLAND,

By W. B. MAC CABE, Esq.

"This work is of great literary value."—TIMES.

"A better book, or more valuable contribution to historical literature, has never been presented to the reading public."—OBSERVER.

"A valuable and extraordinary work."—QUARTERLY REVIEW.

Dedicated, by permission, to EARL GRANVILLE, Lord President of the Committee of Council on Education.

Price 2s. plain, and 2s. 6d. gilt edges.

"OLD SAWS NEWLY SET."

"Earl Granville's recognition of this little book is a certain guarantee of its usefulness and ability. It will cause delight to thousands of young hearts, as well as give a moral tone to thousands of young minds. As a book for schools, and for families educated at home, we can affirm there have been few books published of greater value."—DAILY POST.

"The efficacy and attractiveness of allegory as a means of illustrating great moral truths have been acknowledged in all ages, and Mr. George Linley's genius has done good service in publishing this 'new version of old fables.' This new setting of old saws is well timed and appropriate. Mr. Linley's view is graceful and melodious, and while he tells his familiar stories in a gay and easy manner, he takes care to point their moral with a piquancy and precision not to be misunderstood."—MORNING POST.

Fourth Edition. 4s.

THE BEE-KEEPER'S GUIDE,
By J. H. PAYNE, Esq.

"The best and most concise treatise on the management of bees."—QUARTERLY REVIEW.

In 2 Vols. Price 10s.

SHELLEY AND HIS WRITINGS,
By C. S. MIDDLETON, Esq.

"Never was there a more perfect specimen of biography."—WALTER SAVAGE LANDOR, Esq.

"Mr. Middleton has done good service. He has carefully sifted the sources of information we have mentioned, has made some slight addition, and arranged his materials in proper order and in graceful language. It is the first time the mass of scattered information has been collected and the ground is therefore cleared for a new generation of readers."—ATHENÆUM.

"The life of the poet which has just appeared, and which was much required, is written with much beauty of expression and clearness of purpose. Mr. Middleton's book is a masterly performance."—SOMERSET GAZETTE.

"Mr. Middleton has displayed great ability in following the poet through all the mazes of his life and thoughts. We recommend the work as lively, animated, and interesting. It contains many curious disclosures."—SUNDAY TIMES.

Price 1s. 6d.

PRINCE LIFE,
By G. P. R. JAMES, Esq.,
Author of "The Gipsy," "Richelieu," &c.

"It is worth its weight in gold."—THE GLOBE.

"Most valuable to the rising generation; an invaluable little book"—GUARDIAN.

In 1 Vol. 5s.

STEPS ON THE MOUNTAINS.

"This is a step in the right way, and ought to be in the hands of the youth of both sexes."—REVIEW.

"The moral of this graceful and well-constructed little tale is, that Christian influence and good example may have a better effect in doing the good work of reformation than the prison, the treadmill, or either the reformatory."—CRITIC.

"The Steps on the Mountains are traced in a loving spirit. They are earnest exhortations to the sober and religious-minded to undertake the spiritual and temporal improvement of the condition of the destitute of our lanes and alleys. The moral of the tale is well carried out; and the bread which was cast upon the waters is found after many days, to the saving and happiness of all therein concerned."—ATHENÆUM.

In 1 Vol. 5s.

ALICE SEYMOUR,

By MRS. GRAY.

Author of the "Gambler's Wife," &c.

"A healthy moral tale, such as may be placed in the hands of the young."—DAILY POST.

In 1 Vol., price 7s. 6d.

THE BEAUTIES OF ISAAC BARROW.

"This book is a fitting companion to the 'Beauties of Jeremy Taylor,' and will be useful to the scholars for extracts."—MORNING POST.

In 1 Vol., price 7s. 6d.

THE BEAUTIES OF JEREMY TAYLOR.

"We are bound to say that the collector of Jeremy Taylor's elegant thoughts and aspirations has done his duty successfully. The work will be duly appreciated by the reading public."—EXAMINER.

In 2 Vol. Price 21s.

NAPLES,

By LORD B******M.

In 1 Vol., price 2s. 6d.

CHARADES FOR ACTING.

Mr. Newby's New and Popular Novels.

In 3 Vols. 31s. 6d. (Second Edition).

TRODDEN DOWN,

By MRS. C. J. NEWBY,

Author of "Common Sense," "Kate Kennedy," "Wondrous Strange," &c.

"Mrs. Newby has written several tales of considerable merit, but nothing has come from her pen better than this narrative of woman's trial, error, penitence, and atonement. The reader will peruse 'Trodden Down' with pleasure."—ATHENÆUM.

"'Trodden Down' will firmly establish its author in the same rank as Miss Mulock and the author of 'Adam Bede.'"—GLOBE.

"We have not for a considerable time read a story of so much interest."—OBSERVER.

"We have great pleasure in calling the attention of the reading public to the best novel of the year, 'Trodden Down.'"—HARROGATE ADVERTISER.

"A tale of deep interest, domestic trials, and womanly tenderness, chastened and directed by high moral principles. Mrs. Newby is mistress of the art of connected narrative."—MORNING ADVERTISER.

"The book is a good book, and full of real interest."—CHURCH AND STATE REVIEW.

"The characters are well drawn, the incidents graphically delineated, and the language powerful and graceful."—BRIGHTON EXAMINER.

"The work is a true novel; it is most engrossing in its details, but it is at the same time a really good book, healthy in its morality and sound in its philosophy."—BRIGHTON GAZETTE.

"Mrs. Newby tells her tale with simplicity and feeling, and thus renders it touching and attractive."—LONDON REVIEW.

In 3 Vols.

BEATING TO WINDWARD,

A NOVEL,

By the Honorable C. S. SAVILE,

Author of "Walter Langley," "Leonard Normandale," "Korah Kaplan," &c.

In 2 Vols. 21s.
THE MASTER OF WINGBOURNE.

"One of the very few novels of which it can be said that they would be more acceptable if they were longer. There is great ability shown in the pourtrayal of character. The scenes are thoroughly and forcibly dramatic, and show great power."—MORNING STAR.

"It is a well-written and deeply interesting novel, and the incidents are told with force and cleverness."—OBSERVER.

"The story is well told."—CHURCH AND STATE REVIEW.

"'The Master of Wingbourne' is one of those tales which enforces you to read on and on, a proof that the author writes with a purpose."—MORNING ADVERTISER.

"It is a good novel, and deserves to be freely read."—COURT JOURNAL.

In 3 Vols. 31s. 6d.
OUR BLUE JACKETS
AFLOAT AND ASHORE,
BY F. C. ARMSTRONG,
Author of "The Two Midshipmen," "The Lily of Devon," "The Naval Lieutenant," &c.

"A capital tale for boys."—CHURCH AND STATE REVIEW.

"This novel will be more read and better liked, and give more pleasure to the young of both sexes than any of the numerous Xmas tales which we have seen. It will cheer many a heart."—DAILY POST.

"It is long since we have read so thoroughly interesting a book as this. There is no doubt this novel will become a great favorite with the public, as it is written to interest men as well as the usual readers of such books."—OBSERVER.

"Mr. Armstrong, in 'Our Blue Jackets,' has even exceeded in style his well-written novel of 'The Naval Lieutenant,' and given us one continued series of interesting and thrilling incidents. It will compare with 'Midshipman Easy,' without losing thereby."—READER.

"Not one of our celebrated naval novelists ever wrote a better tale than 'Our Blue Jackets.' There is no modern fiction that will afford more pleasure to readers of both sexes."—HARROGATE ADVERTISER.

"Mr. Armstrong stands unrivalled as a writer of sea tales; 'Our Blue Jackets' is by far the best, and by far the most interesting novel he has written His descriptions of Spanish life and customs give it a peculiar interest. It will be a great favorite with lady readers."—HERALD.

In 2 Vols.
THROWN ON THE WORLD.

"The book is readable, and free from all objectionable matter. The author desires to show not what trouble is, but the readiest and most practicable way of getting out of it, or the best and most cheerful way of bearing it."—ATHENÆUM.

"This is a well-written and most interesting story of domestic life, which will commend itself to all lovers of works of fiction of a moral and elevating character."—BRIGHTON EXAMINER.

"This is a pleasing story, in which the battle of life is fought by strong wills and energetic minds."—OBSERVER.

"A novel pure and simple."—CHURCH AND STATE REVIEW.

In 2 Vols. 21s.

THE STORY OF NELLY DILLON,

By the Author of "Myself and my Relatives."

"It is written with the finished simplicity of an experienced storyist, and its traits of Irish life and modes of Irish thoughts and expression are like daguerreotypes in their exactness and exquisite expression."—DUBLIN GENERAL ADVERTISER.

"A vigorous tale, most true in its sketches of Irish life. This story must have been written by a person thoroughly familiar with the modes of thought, and forms of speech which characterise the Irish peasantry."—WARDER.

"Graphic and life-like."—DAILY EXPRESS.

"A vigorous tale, most true in its sketches of Irish life."—DUBLIN EVENING PACKET.

"The novel is written with spirit, and the language is enlivened with considerable wit and humour."—OBSERVER.

"'Nelly Dillon' is unapproachably excellent."—LONDON REVIEW.

"Well told, and full of interest; altogether a superior book."—CHURCH AND STATE REVIEW.

In 2 Vols. 21s.

LANDMARKS OF A LIFE,

A NOVEL,

By B. C. AUSTIN.

"The name of Austin ranks high in the literary annals of England, and B. C. Austin will add another link to its honour. 'Landmarks of a Life' is written gracefully, and the tale is one of great interest."—DAILY EXAMINER.

In 2 Vols.

LOST AT THE WINNING POST.

A NOVEL,

By H. L. STEVENSON, cousin of the late W. M. Thackeray,

Author of "A Heart Twice Won."

In 2 Vols. 21s.

THE CHEPFORD PEOPLE,
A STORY ABOUT THEMSELVES, THEIR PASTORS, MASTERS, AND NEIGHBOURS.

In 3 Vols.

NEW NOBILITY.
A NOVEL.

In 2 Vols., 21s.

LILIAN'S INHERITANCE.
A NOVEL,
By Mrs. WILLIAM MURRAY.

SECOND EDITION.

In 3 Vols.

AN OLD MAN'S SECRET,
By FRANK TROLLOPE.

"As a picture of English country life, with charming development of character, a highly moral tone, and a story of powerful interest, this novel will take rank with the very best of our English fictions."—GLOBE.

"The portraiture of Dr. Weatherby would not have been unworthy the pen of Oliver Goldsmith."—DAILY POST.

"This novel has pith, vigour, and freshness. The story never flags."—MORNING ADVERTISER.

"There is a very decided originality about this novel. It is due to Mr. Trollope to state that he has worked out the intricacies of an elaborate plot very ingeniously. The author of such a story must undoubtedly possess a large share of imagination, and he has powers of descriptive writing to an equal extent. We leave this novel to bear the public test, confident that it will make its way into the favour of a discriminating public."—OBSERVER.

"Certainly one of the best novels of the present year."—MORNING HERALD.

"The characters are not only consistent and natural, but really interesting studies of probable personages."—MANCHESTER GUARDIAN.

"It is a book which inculcates a rather good view of society, and may be safely placed in the hands of all classes of readers."—COURT CIRCULAR.

In 3 Vols.

THE DAUGHTER OF CATHERWOOD,

By Mrs. KELLY

(DAUGHTER OF MRS. SHERWOOD).

In 2 Vols.

MY SISTER DAGMAR.

By the Author of "Uncle Clive."

In 2 Vols. 21s.

SHOT!

By F. SHERIDAN.

"The plot is worked out, and a most interesting tale is well-evolved from it. It is a deeply interesting romance."—OBSERVER.

"We have seldom met with a story told so spiritedly. The heroine's passionate love for Lord Sturdith is delightfully depicted. The poaching gipsy is a capital character, whose daring adventures are told by Mr. Sheridan with suitable *eclat*."—PRESS.

"The story is well narrated."—READER.

"Vivid descriptions, clothed in fresh and agreable language, prove the ability of the writer. Mr. Sheridan succeeds in securing the interest of his readers."—PUBLIC OPINION.

In 3 Vols.

UNCLE ARMSTRONG,

By LORD B * * * * * * M,

Author of "Masters and Workmen."

"The style is simple and easy."—READER.

In Three Vols.

MAGGIE LYNNE,

By ALTON CLYDE,

Author of "Tried and True," &c.

"There are many characters of interest in the novel, and the various scenes are written with talent."—OBSERVER.

"We can honestly praise this novel."—MANCHESTER GUARDIAN.

"A story of strong character and deep domestic sympathies. No novel reader will be able to lay down these volumes till 'Maggie Lynne' has become Mrs. Paul Dillon. We have not lately taken up a work which is better calculated to wile away a quiet afternoon."—MORNING ADVERTISER.

"Sound in tone, enforcing by precept and example sentiments which are calculated to produce salutary effects on the mind of the young."—BIRMINGHAM ADVERTISER.

"There are few writers of fiction who have trespassed so near to the 'wild and thrilling' incidents of the 'legitimate' novel with the same clever avoidance of what is unreal and inartistic as the author of 'Tried and True,' in his present work, 'Maggie Lynne.' Where many have failed, the author of 'Maggie Lynne' has secured a fairly earned triumph. The diction is pure, the characters natural, and the construction of the plot clever; it is no wonder then that the author has succeeded in making 'Maggie Lynne' at once a charming and entertaining novel."—PUBLIC OPINION.

"The author shows constructive power and much cleverness in the delineation of character, with an easy, agreeable style."—SHARPE'S MAGAZINE.

In 3 Vols. 31s. 6d.

THE GAIN OF A LOSS,

A NOVEL,

By the Author of "The Last of the Cavaliers."

"The story is well told, and the suspense, the constant change from hope to despair at first, and the final triumph of despair forms a most touching part in this history of a true and faithful love."—OBSERVER.

"The author of 'The Last of the Cavaliers' is known to a numerous body of readers, and this new book, so far from disappointing her friends, will give them additional pleasure and fresh reasons for their admiration of a truly talented writer."—MANCHESTER GUARDIAN.

"An excellent novel, in every way worthy of the reputation of the author of 'The Last of the Cavaliers.' For grace, delicacy, and dramatic skill, we have read few things so good in the novels that have recently been in our hands."—LONDON REVIEW.

"The book is pervaded by an excellent spirit."—ATHENÆUM.

In 1 Vol. 10s. 6d.

ADVENTURES OF A SERF'S WIFE AMONG THE MINES OF SIBERIA.

"In this volume the reader will find a very graphic and truthful idea of the physical condition of a large portion of Russia and its people."—OBSERVER.

"A better idea of the inner parts of Russia may be derived from reading this single volume than from any works of travel."—LONDON REVIEW.

"The story is of deep interest, while the charming sketches of Russian peasant life are deserving of great praise."—PUBLIC OPINION.

"'The Serf's Wife' might aspire to be reckoned among works of history."—CHURCH AND STATE REVIEW.

In 1 Vol. 10s. 6d.

ASHTON MORTON,

A NOVEL.

"Both honest and well meant. Its pages do not contain the faintest suggestion of 'sensationalism.' They breathe throughout an air of genuine, every-day religion."—ATHENÆUM

"The author has evidently sketched her *dramatis personæ* from life; her models have been carefully and judiciously chosen. We heartily commend 'Ashton Morton' to the perusal of those who desire to meet in the pages of fiction characters and incidents of every day life. There are many characters in it it will not be easy to forget."—PUBLIC OPINION.

In 2 Vols. 21s.

A HEART TWICE WON,

BY H. L. STEVENSON.

Dedicated (by permission of his daughter) to her cousin, the late W. M. Thackeray.

"The characters are limned with a steady pencil, and the colouring dashed in with broad lights."—WORCESTER HERALD.

"A simple story pleasantly told."—BELL'S MESSENGER.

"It will be read with the liveliest interest."—PUBLIC OPINION.

In 3 Vols. 31s. 6d.

A TROUBLED STREAM,

By the Author of "The Cliffords of Oakley."

"The story is told with much taste."—BELL'S MESSENGER.

"It is a pretty story."—OBSERVER.

FOURTH EDITION.

In Three Vols.

COMMON SENSE,

A NOVEL,

By the Author of "Trodden Down."

"To read common sense in a novel is a very uncommon thing, but to find three volumes of common sense is perfectly surprising; yet such is the case with Mrs. Newby's last work. Every chapter contains an instructive lesson in life, an object set before us to acquire, and the means of obtaining it by the most upright and honourable means. It may with safety be recommended as an admirable novel."—OBSERVER.

"We have read this novel with pleasure. It is a healthy, sensible, and interesting story. The title is sober, and scarcely indicates the high order of qualities which are illustrated in the narrative—a story which may be read with profit as well as pleasure."—ATHENÆUM.

"We predicted that 'Kate Kennedy' would be the precursor of still higher achievements, and we have not been disappointed. It can with advantage be put into the hands of the youngest novel reader, who may learn from it that the smallest affairs in life may be regulated by the highest principles."—VICTORIA MAGAZINE.

"The whole tone of the book is healthy, the style is easy, and the language well chosen. The love scenes are far more true to life than the sickly sentimentalities we are often invited to accept as heart effusions. The story is built on one great evil of the present day, the living beyond one's means, and we would particularly call attention to the good feeling which is shown as existing between the different classes of society. The plot is simple and natural. It is one of the best novels of the day, the healthy tone of which will place it on the same shelf with those of Miss Austen."—READER.

In 2 Vols. (This Day).

HETTY GOULDWORTH,

A NOVEL.

By GEORGE MACAULAY.

"The author writes easily, elegantly, and picturesquely."—MANCHESTER GUARDIAN.

In Three Vols.

ALL ABOUT THE MARSDENS.

A NOVEL.

"An interesting story told with truly feminine delicacy. It is sure to become popular."—OBSERVER.

"The reader who can appreciate home details, charming development of loving natures, kindly sympathies, and small errors of the head—but not of the heart—will peruse this work from the commencement to the close with pleasure and profit."—BELL'S MESSENGER.

"An interesting tale of pure domestic life, very pleasantly written, is this story of the 'Marsdens.' Life, its aim and ends, are earnestly dealt with, and grave lessons are thus naturally engendered. It is a perfectly moral and well-considered story, and will prove safe and pleasant reading for our young people."—COURT CIRCULAR.

"Mrs. Waller writes gracefully and agreeably; her characters are true to nature, and carefully drawn. The story is one eminently suited for young lady readers. Nothing can be purer than the tone and teaching of the story."—SHARPE'S MAGAZINE.

"It presents talent of no common order."—PUBLIC OPINION.

In Three Vols.

IT MAY BE TRUE,

A NOVEL,

By MRS. WOOD.

"A highly interesting novel."—OBSERVER.

"'It may be True' is a novel good enough in all respects to warrant us in recommending our readers to read it. It is clever, spirited, sensible, and interesting, and when powerful writing, or vivid description, or genuine humour is wanted, Mrs. Wood is equal to all those occasions."—ATHENÆUM.

In 3 Vols. 31s. 6d.

THE MAITLANDS,

A NOVEL,

By the Author of "Three Opportunities."

"Each chapter is a homily; every volume contains a world of good advice. The strictest parent might rejoice to see his daughter poring over its pages."—LONDON REVIEW.

In Three Vols.

TREASON AT HOME.
A NOVEL.

"It is somewhat remarkable to open a new novel and to find it possesses so much interest and so many striking qualities as 'Treason at Home.' It is written with great ease and power."—COURT CIRCULAR.

"This is a well-written, interesting story, which we can safely recommend. We congratulate the author on her success. Lady Tremyss is a well-sketched character, carefully filled in, and the fascination which is intended to surround her is plainly felt by the reader. 'Treason at Home' is a very superior novel."—OBSERVER.

"It is a long time since we have met with a work of fiction possessing so much freshness and originality."—COURT JOURNAL.

IN THE PRESS.

IN JANUARY—1867.

MRS. WOOD'S NEW NOVEL,

IN THREE VOLS.,

SIR CYRUS OF STONYCLEFT.

IN FEBRUARY.

MR. F. TROLLOPE'S NEW TALE

THE RIVAL DOCTORS.

www.ingramcontent.com/pod-product-compliance
Lightning Source LLC
Chambersburg PA
CBHW032149230426
43672CB00011B/2493